MW00334006

Steven Morris's new book, *The Beautiful Business*, is a must-read manifesto for 21st century business leaders. Morris lays out a vision for a new type of business along with the practical skills for building it. I found the book engaging, thought-provoking, and a pleasure to read. Highly recommended.

Gay Hendricks, PhD, author of *The Big Leap: Conquer Your Hidden Fear and Take Life to the Next Level* and *The Genius Zone: The Breakthrough Process to End Negative Thinking and Live in True Creativity*

It's time to bring love to the business world and Steven Morris is taking a courageous stand to remind us all that people want so much more than paychecks and titles. They want the full engagement that comes when they are aligned with beauty, love, and meaning. I am very excited about this refreshing look at leadership and business, and trust you will, too.

Diana Chapman, cofounder of Conscious Leadership Group and coauthor of the bestselling book *The 15 Commitments of Conscious Leadership: A New Paradigm for Sustainable Success*

In *The Beautiful Business*, Steven Morris speaks in terms rarely applied to business, beauty, soul, truth, and evolution. What this book shows is how the work of business can evolve into the craft of business and ultimately into the art of business and business leadership. Steven has masterfully articulated a path to follow that allows business leaders to bring their full self into the business and to encourage those who work with them to do the same to create a sense of purpose and belonging that transcends metrics and profits.

Jim Canfield, president of CEO Tools by Aprio and author of *CEO Tools 2.0: A System to Think, Manage, and Lead Like a CEO*

Business as usual is broken. Conscious leaders know there is a better way to honor people *and* profits, but don't always have the tools to teach team members how. *The Beautiful Business* is a wise beacon illuminating a new way forward. With heart and soul, combined with his decades of experience as an executive and entrepreneur, Steven Morris offers an invitation to lead with artistry, creativity, and fierce pragmatism—all while producing abundant, tangible results. May businesses everywhere begin their journey toward *unignorable* beauty, purpose, and impact, with this powerful guide as their compass.

Jenny Blake, author of *Pivot* and *Free Time: Lose The Busywork, Love Your Business*

The Beautiful Business offers a completely fresh take on creating a business that matters. This actionable manifesto is sure to inspire, inform, and ignite the fire at the heart of your business. You will be better for reading this book.

Dorie Clark, author of *Entrepreneurial You* and executive education faculty for Duke University Fuqua School of Business

It reads like a new bible for the business leader who wants a wholehearted life and a valuable business. Beautifully designed and accessible, *The Beautiful Business* invites business owners to take charge of reinventing capitalism from a winner-takes-most or never-enough mentality into something sacred that celebrates business as a form of service. If you've read other books about business and still felt like something was missing, this is the book you've been waiting for.

Leisa Peterson, author of *The Mindful Millionaire*

Profound! Every once in a while, a book comes along that challenges the very core of my thinking about business. *The Beautiful Business* did just that. It opened my eyes to the creative journey that building and running a company is, and how letting go of a conventional leadership approach and seeing and acting with artistry, conviction, and love can transform our businesses and ourselves. Read this book if you want to think deeply about the potential for business today and then create something valuable, sustainable, and beautiful.

> **Denise Lee Yohn**, author of *What Great Brands Do: The Seven Brand-Building Principles that Separate the Best from the Rest* and *Fusion: How Integrating Brand and Culture Powers the World's Greatest Companies*

The Beautiful Business reveals Steven Morris's view of business as an act of creation on a daily basis. It calls each of us pursuing such a creation to express our higher selves for the good of the whole. It is a mirror to our soul, and, as you read it, you will see the beauty in you which empowers you to create your *beautiful business*.

> **Gene Early, PhD**, partner of Leader's Quest and author of *3 Keys to Transforming Your Potential*

Part Simon Sinek, part Abraham Maslow, part Picasso— *The Beautiful Business* is a thought-provoking and practical guide to build more meaning and magnetism into your business. Steven Morris's book breaks new ground in business thinking.

> **Chip Conley**, founder of Modern Elder Academy and author of *Wisdom at Work: The Making of a Modern Elder*, *Emotional Equations: Simple Truths for Creating Happiness + Success*, and *Peak: How Great Companies Get their Mojo from Maslow*

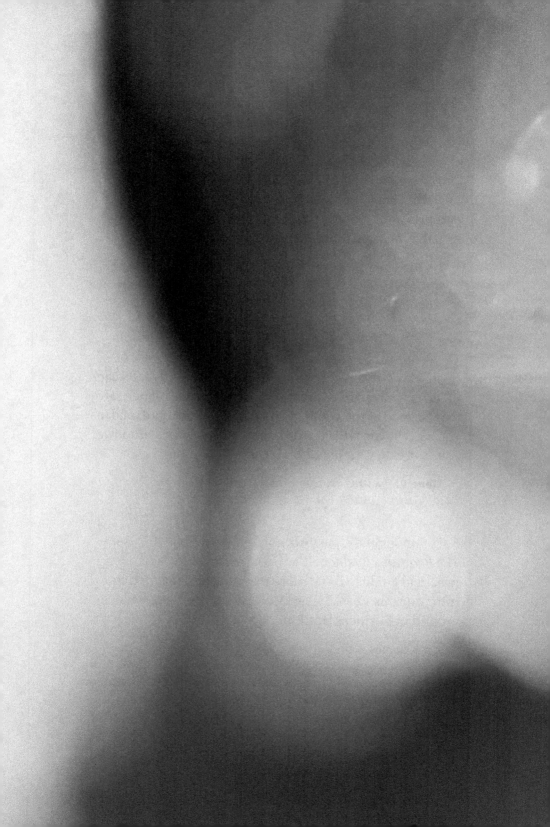

An Actionable Manifesto to
Create an Unignorable
Business with Love at the Core

The
Beautiful
Business

Steven Morris

CONSCIOUS
CAPITALISM
PRESS™

 **Conscious Capitalism Press**
www.consciouscapitalism.org/press

 Round Table Companies
Packaging, production, and distribution services
www.roundtablecompanies.com

Deerfield, IL

Executive Editing	**Agata Antonow**
Cover Design	**Steven Morris, Sunny DiMartino**
Photography	**Steven Morris**
Infographics	**Steven Morris**
Interior Design	**Christy Bui, Sunny DiMartino, Steven Morris**
Proofreading	**Adam Lawrence, Carly Cohen**

Printed in the United States of America

First Edition: November 2021
10 9 8 7 6 5 4 3 2 1

Library of Congress Cataloging-in-Publication Data
The beautiful business: an actionable manifesto to create an unignorable business with love at the core / Steven Morris.—1st ed. p. cm.
ISBN Hardcover: 978-1-950466-28-3
ISBN Digital: 978-1-950466-29-0
Library of Congress Control Number: 2021943993

Conscious Capitalism Press is an imprint of Conscious Capitalism, Inc. The Conscious Capitalism Press logo is a trademark of Conscious Capitalism, Inc.

Round Table Companies and the RTC logo are trademarks of Writers of the Round Table, Inc.

The
Beautiful
Business

Prelude

One of the things I have learned about being in business is that there are no set rules. There are no must-dos, other than to survive, and even that's mostly a choice. Much of what business schools, business leaders, and business books teach is cut from the fabric of experiences that come through the trials and errors of doing business.

Of course, there are loads of historical data harvested from successful and unsuccessful businesses that can and should be studied and learned from. But how one great company realized success or how some failed is not necessarily the right approach for your business, and it's no guarantee of success or failure. Just because another company succeeds or fails doesn't define your path to success or even your fulfillment. Life and business are a grand experiment—an open canvas, a blank page, and an empty vessel for you to fill with your passions, drivers, desires, and dreams. It's all a journey into the abyss of what's possible.

On the other side of surviving in business is a playing field of flourishing. It's the *world of possibilities*. As the term suggests, in this world, anything is possible and everything is waiting for you. While we may not call it that, it's the world that most entrepreneurs live and work in. This world is daunting for some and utterly creative for others. I invite you to see and treat the world of business—your business—as the experimentation that it is: a meaningful experiment in value creation designed to explore not only what's possible for your business and the people it serves, but what's possible for you.

However, as you'll see within the chapters and pages that follow, this world of possibilities operates best when boundaries and a framework are installed for you to be creative. No business leader, no maker, no artist has a boundless world in which they work. Just as an artist needs to master the tools and techniques of the craft, the edge of a canvas, a motivating purpose to paint, and an audience to reach, a business leader needs a set of defined guidelines through which they can create their business, make decisions, and define success.

When a leader defines their business's higher purpose, they begin that edge- and direction-defining journey. We know there's a world of difference between a job, a career, and a calling. What's less discussed is the chasm one must cross to get from one stage to the next. For some, it's fine to stay in the job zone or the career zone. You can make a fruitful and happy life out of any job or career. But a calling is something else entirely.

The same could be said about a company. The company that's operating for the money and money alone is a far cry from the business that's committed to a higher purpose. This is the central thesis to this book: an actionable manifesto for the business leader who wants to transition your business into a calling—a calling for you, your employees, and your customers.

This book is for the entrepreneur who wants to live a life of wholehearted examination through their business. It's for the businessperson who is brave enough to shape a new reality that's worth shaping—one that evolves into a calling. It's for the people who are committed to living and working with a liberated heart. It's for the leader who wants an unignorable business that sustains itself from an inner force for as long as you can envision.

One person, in early comments about this book, referred to it as "*The Artist's Way* for business leaders." While I certainly don't claim the greatness or lasting impact of Julia Cameron's seminal book, I do align with this assessment in one fashion that *The Beautiful Business* is intended to shine a light on a more vital way to think about and do business. It's a way to think of yourself as a gardener that plants meaningful seeds inside your business, and nurtures and grows them into a flourishing venture. It's a way of doing business that tethers a business leader's intrinsic higher-purpose drivers to their creative applications in the world of their business. Like Julia's book, this book is an invitation to investigate, experiment, do the daily work, and cultivate a life in business as a grand experiment in a creatively serious fashion. I invite you to see this book as a light, a beacon, and a calling. I'm glad you're here with me for the adventure.

> **❝ Out beyond ideas of wrongdoing and rightdoing, there is a field. I'll meet you there.**
>
> — RUMI

Orienting Your Book Journey

I get it, this is an unusual book. And, I suspect that you might be a little unusual, too. Just like me. Let's face it, you have to be a little strange to embark upon the abyss of entrepreneurship and leadership. But, your unusual, your weird, your crazy is part of what makes *you* uniquely *you*. And most likely, it's what makes you great.

So, instead of trying to keep up some perfect picture of someone else's vision of you, you can own your weird. You are trying to move your business and your world further. You are expanding reality. Most criticism of you, your business, or your ideas will come from people who are judging you based on their world view or a very narrow view of reality. It's hard for others to make sense of your vision and purpose. You don't owe anyone an explanation for your uniqueness. Your birthright is to be fully and completely you. Your business has that birthright, too.

Of course, you're not alone. In fact, you're in pretty good company. As the now-famous "Crazy Ones" Apple ad from 1997 proclaimed:

Here's to the crazy ones.
The misfits.
The rebels.
The troublemakers.
The round pegs in the square holes.

The ones who see things differently.

They're not fond of rules.
And they have no respect for the status quo.

You can quote them, disagree with them,
glorify or vilify them.
About the only thing you can't do is ignore them.

Because they change things.

They push the human race forward.

While some may see them as the crazy ones,
we see genius.

Because the people who are crazy enough to think
they can change the world, are the ones who do.

In order to help orient you on what you're about to embark upon, I've outlined a map for your journey ahead. I invite you to see this as a treasure map for discovering your own unique unusual artistry as you think about and adventure yourself through your beautiful business trajectory.

The Road Ahead

Manifesto
for the Beautiful Business

Chapter **1.**
Entrepreneur
as Maker,
Craftsman,
Artist

Chapter **2.**
Why a
**Beautiful
Business?**

Chapter **3.**
The
**Business
Evolution**

Chapter **4.**
Tenets
of the
Beautiful Business

The Beautiful Business / Journey
Table of Contents

The Road Ahead

I've shaped this book as a series of building blocks intended to set a solid foundation on which to build, grow, and amplify your beautiful business. I have found that principles are better than direct rules or instructions and that questions are our greatest avenue to framing and investigating how information can apply and be relevant to our work. Each section of this book is framed, in part, by the investigation into questions that have helped me and other leaders I've worked with. As such, the structure of this book follows this path.

This book is organized into two major sections. Building on the artist metaphor stated in the prelude, this first section, which includes chapters 1–5, is focused on priming and defining the framework for your beautiful business. The second section, which includes chapters 6–9, is focused on tending to your business work of art, so your business will flourish. So first I'll talk about what a beautiful business is, why it matters, and how it works, then I'll share insights into building it.

The only
constant in
the universe
is change.

— HERACLITUS

The Manifesto for the Beautiful Business

❝ Every noble work is at first impossible.

— THOMAS CARLYLE

A Business Values Revolution

The course of modern events has led us to a time and a place where the highest angels of our nature are called to step forward. This time and place slices urgent as an arrow. The greed of consumerism and materialism has steered us to a course where *things* are valued over *people*, where we are combating our fellow humans, where workplace dysfunction has heightened our collective anxiety, and where the disease of busyness has eroded our ability to be present in our personal relationships.

This movement toward a more beautiful form of capitalism is not shaped by the reactions to agitations that demand so much from us but rather by what we are courageous enough to give to the world. What is the degree of our audacity to offer the best version of our businesses so that it benefits the wholeness of our humanity?

Once, the world was flat. Once, the earth was the center of our solar system. Or so we thought. There will be another intellectual leap that takes place when enough of us come to the embodied realization that we are all inextricably connected to one another and to all things.

The idea that the progression of our human existence—beginning with the ancient and primitive through modern times—is naturally going to continue to ever greater heights is a slippery illusion. We are complicit in the world we live in. We are participating in a grand experiment, where the likes of technology and accumulation of human skills has led to significant destruction. This includes environmental destruction and depletion, weapons of war that can desecrate entire cities, and social technologies that have increased depression and suicide, to name a few. This is not because technology or advanced human skills are inherently bad but rather because the attitude in which we have applied these assets has been in the spirit of humans against humans, humans against nature, and humans against the universe. We have to realize that we are an integral part of nature, just as much as any other natural thing or being. When we lack this realization of our interconnectedness, we use our powers to destroy our fellow humans and the environment.

> **❝ Our task must be to free ourselves . . . by widening our circle of compassion to embrace all living creatures and the whole of nature and its beauty.**
>
> — ALBERT EINSTEIN

However, when enough of us know the truth of our interconnectedness, we will then use our technologies, skill advancement, and economic engines in ways that reinforce and amplify that interconnectedness.

Jacqueline Novogratz, CEO of Acumen and author of *Manifesto for a Moral Revolution*, speaks about this interconnectedness in terms of *accompaniment*. In her book, she writes, "This is the secret of accompaniment. I will hold a mirror to you and show you your value, bear witness to your suffering, and to your light. And over time, you will do the same for me, for within the relationship lies the promise of our shared dignity and the mutual encouragement needed to do the hard things." She continues: "Whatever you aim to do, whatever problem you hope to address, remember to accompany those who are struggling, those who are left out, who lack the capabilities needed to solve their own problems. We are each other's destiny. Beneath the hard skills and firm strategic priorities needed to resolve our greatest challenges lies the soft, fertile ground of our shared humanity. In that place of hard and soft is sustenance enough to nourish the entire human family."

This shared humanity starts with your leadership—
with your evolved realization that we are all made from the
lineage that came before us, and that we make ourselves
and our businesses out of the fabric of possibilities that
lie ahead. We, personally and professionally, are always
in the process of evolving into our possibilities when our
intention is well aimed. The urgent calling of modern time
is to recast, reimagine, and reshape our business as a tool
to facilitate our integrated wholeness rather than fortify
our separation.

There will be some that think or say that I'm crazy and
that you're crazy, too. All edge-pushers are considered
crazy by those who grasp with fear the things that they
believe are keeping them moored to their perceived
safety. You might as well see the beautiful business for
the revolution that it is. Those that resist change and live
within the limiting motto of "it's always been done this
way" are the ones who find themselves clawing to catch
up to a world that's surpassed them or, worse, become
irrelevant as they cling to the past.

Manifesting Beauty

There is a revolution afoot. A rumbling.
A groundswell. A quiet tsunami. We've
reached levels of such abundance
in many parts of our society that our
attention can be attuned to aims
that go beyond survival and security.
Business leaders and entrepreneurs
are evolving into the fusion of ideas
that, with the abundance of these
times, there is an opportunity to serve
and help humanity in larger ways.
Certainly, there is the awareness that
life is finite and uncertain, precious and
unpredictable, fleeting and abundant
with possibility. People just like you
and I are acting on the realization that
life is a precious gift, and our positions
in leadership, regardless of our role or
size of the business, are a stewardship
responsibility to care for people
and planet.

There is, directly in front of us, the ripe and fertile opportunity to form and lead our businesses through what Dr. Martin Luther King Jr. described as the "beautiful struggle." While Dr. King was describing the yet-to-be-resolved beautiful struggle of racism, I humbly borrow this term and apply it to the beautiful business journey: the striving to apply our amassed skills, technologies, and economies for the good of an integrated system of working, growing, evolving, and living.

Again, here I want to reinforce that I am humbly borrowing the "beautiful struggle" from Rev. Dr. Martin Luther King, Jr., with the full acknowledgment that the challenges of racial and civil rights are nowhere close to being settled. The need in our society, our economy, and our business cultures for justice, equality, diversity, and inclusion (JEDI) is essential if our business systems are to be whole. As the saying goes, if you want to go fast go alone, but if you want to go far go together.

If you're reading this book, I assume you are interested in being an active participant in a world-changing movement to evolve businesses that will solve big and small problems. Maybe you run a small start-up or are in charge of a massive global team. Maybe you're an activist entrepreneur. Maybe you're running a nonprofit. Maybe you're a solopreneur, a budding entrepreneur, or the leader of a team within a larger organization. If any of those apply, this book, and the calling within it, is for you. I have witnessed firsthand the good that businesses and their leaders can do to be a positive force for change. I have seen people like you improve the environment, alter the education of children and students, serve the underprivileged, and create products and services that improve the lives of millions. I have seen you in the beautiful struggle to do good and succeed.

There are three myths that I'd like to dispel here and now.

Myth #1: Wealth = bad person. In our society, many people will assume that "You're a bad person because you're wealthy."

Self-aware people make better leaders. Of course, not all wealthy people and leaders are self-aware people. The news headlines are full of powerful leaders who've been toppled by the exposure of their misdeeds. These examples of unhealthy leaders of the world leave a stain on good people and business leaders who have built exceptionally profitable businesses while doing good for people and planet in the way they generated their profit.

Author of *Atomic Habits* James Clear notes that "wealth is the power to choose. Financial wealth is the power to choose how to spend money . . . Time wealth is the power to choose how to spend your day. Mental wealth is the power to choose how to spend your attention."[1] I'll add that leadership wealth is the power to wield your position for the good of the whole.

You alone are the only person alive who has the power to choose how to spend your life; each day, each dollar, each decision, each action. Your capacity to choose is your power and your wealth. Your career path, job, leadership approach, the business you create, the impact that you intend to create are all yours for the choosing. The character that arises from your beliefs defines your level of goodness. The size of your business profit or bank account says nothing about the goodness of your character.

Myth #2: Nonprofit or B Corp leaders aren't serious about business. The false assumption is that "if you're running a nonprofit or a B Corp, it's because you don't know how to manage for profit." Both nonprofit and B Corps are different and unique legal business structures. While they are not the same, the founders or leaders of each type of organization have made a conscious commitment to doing business with measured outcomes that go beyond profit or profit alone.

Social entrepreneurship, for those who know anything about this approach to business, is a difficult path that is often driven by a higher calling. Building a business for profit only is, frankly, the easy route. Courageous leaders engage in the *both/and of profit and purpose, of doing well by doing good*. And you don't have to run a nonprofit or even a B Corp to run a beautiful business and make a positive impact on the world around you. No, that good work happens not with the structure of your company but with the higher purpose infused within it.

Myth #3: Artistry = frivolity. The world of business is often allergic to the artistic side of business, often bowing to the altar of data over instinct. When some businesspeople think about artists or artistry, they're often envisioning a beret-wearing creative with their head in the clouds who doesn't easily fit within the confinement of business considerations. Yet, outside the world of business, so much valuable thinking and creativity is sought out and embraced in the moving mastery of artistry to shape and change societies. Great artists are marks of great cultures. Artists, craftspeople, and artisans call what is produced a work of art. A work of art can be defined as something that transcends a person's earned technical skills and produces a work that is beyond ordinary craftsmanship. As such, a work of art literally moves the audience.

Evolved business actions come from leading your life with your heart and soul front and center. The artistry of living and leading enlivens the tether to your heart and soul simply because human artistry comes from the heart and soul. The best of business leaders have a bias toward action that enlivens them and those around them. This is living artistry: a movement inward to your highest values that then extends outward to move the world around you through your inspired action.

What's in It for You?

So, what's in it for you, the business leader? I don't have to tell you how challenging it is to launch, build, lead, and grow your business. You live with this reality every day, even when you're not at work. Entrepreneurship is not for the faint of heart. Some might point out that it's for people who are a little bit or a lot obsessed. Maybe you're obsessed or maybe just impassioned to create something of value on your terms. Maybe you're simply sick and tired of the old guard of business that treats humans as a resource commodity and customers as suckers. Maybe you've made a ton of money and have climbed the golden mountain only to look at the view and wonder, what now? If you're like me, at some point—likely on your darkest, most challenging days—you'll ask yourself out loud, "Is it all worth it?" or "Why am I doing this?"

While launching, building, and growing my business, I've passed through some challenging junctures; remembering, for instance, 9/11 or the recession of 2008. I in fact wrote this book in part while much of the world was locked down from the COVID-19 pandemic. Each of these were cataclysmic events that were completely out of my control yet still had profound effects on my business and nearly all others. On these most darkened of days, I looked inside myself for motivations to stride ahead into, as Dante put it, "the middle of my life, where the way forward was wholly lost."

This book is written to shepherd your business, with brilliance, guts, and grace, through your darkest and lightest days. It's created for the care and nurturing of business leaders who have a sense that what they're doing could be more impactful and exponentially more valuable.

Consider the ideas and strategies of *The Beautiful Business* as a launchpad for your business and your brand; you don't need to deploy everything offered within this book to build a beautiful business and be successful. However, you'll find that the more you apply the thinking and approaches within, the more you'll deepen your driving reason for being as a business, foster your leadership team alignment, ignite your employee engagement, build your loyal brand following, and grow your top and bottom lines. Regardless of the strategies and tactics you choose, the most critical aspect is taking the first step—and building your beautiful business on purpose.

Investing in You

You frankly owe it to your life to strive to be the best version of yourself you can be. This debt is owed to all you do in your work, your business, and your life. Part of your responsibility as a business leader and entrepreneur is to create the best, most vital, most valuable, most beneficial version of your business that you can create. This is not a fanciful aspiration. It's a purposeful and actionable intent to create a living work of art that attempts to rise to the immeasurable gift of life.

Down deep in the hearts and souls of the wisest of people, they know that by helping others thrive, flourish, and live to the fullest, they help themselves. Life is full of uncertainty. Each day we step into, we know not what will come and what life will bring. Each day is a risk. Each work a venture. Despite our systematized efforts to envision and shape the unfolding of events as orderly, managed, and fixed, we do not know what will happen next. Not today, not tomorrow.

I believe in conscious evolution. I believe in the unity of all things. I believe in imaginative doors that open to a wide and wild future. I believe in the power for good people to shape and reshape the world of business, economies, and cultures that bends with the arc of time toward the inextricable unity of all things, seen and unseen. I believe in doing what must be done to course correct the trajectory of our past doings.

As we sit atop the food chain, we inherit a stewardship responsibility to act for the good of the whole. We may not have asked for this leadership position, but here we are, in charge of our own destiny and the destiny of our planet and people. If the world crashes and burns, it won't matter who's to blame because there will be no history books left to point the finger at the wrongdoers. The antidote to our ills is to pollinate our highest nature of goodness.

We must give in order to get. We must love in order to be loved. In order to shine, we must bear the ability to burn. No one escapes life without bruises or broken parts. No one thrives without struggle. Comfort is overrated. The *beautiful struggle* that Dr. King describes refers to the ability to burn our light in the presence of those who have yet to face it. Those of you who do or aim to lead, your job is to courageously enter this *beautiful struggle*, and to help others shine along the way. You are here to shine, my friends.

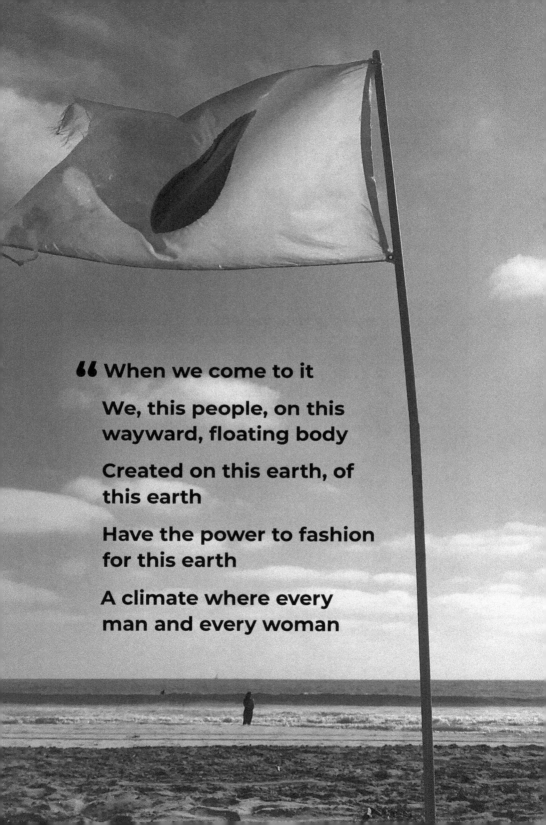

66 When we come to it

We, this people, on this
wayward, floating body

Created on this earth, of
this earth

Have the power to fashion
for this earth

A climate where every
man and every woman

Can live freely without
sanctimonious piety

Without crippling fear

When we come to it

We must confess that we
are the possible

We are the miraculous, the
true wonder of this world

That is when, and only when

We come to it.

— MAYA ANGELOU, "A BRAVE AND STARTLING TRUTH"

Rising Above the Noise: Beyond Binary Thinking

I can look out at the wide horizon of the vast Pacific Ocean on a pristine day in the surf, and I'm reminded that this horizon isn't nearly as flat as I perceive it. There beyond the vast ocean is a curvature that I cannot see around. Beyond that is a vast sea of space that stretches beyond the imaginable. Yet I know this oceanic image is an illusion that curves around an arc on a spinning, wobbling blue marble that orbits a great sun. This vast ocean is a mote on the lands we inhabit. Just as our spinning planet is a tiny island suspended by gravity in a vast universe.

On December 7, 1972, a great data point was captured in the tiny window on the Apollo 17 aircraft through the lens of a 70-millimeter Hasselblad Data Camera. The now-famous photo "The Blue Marble Shot" was one of four shots taken that day of the whole Earth. The data point demonstrated what we already knew—the Earth was round. But it showed so much more if you look beyond the image. Carl Sagan, the famed astronomer and writer, wrote

The Pale Blue Dot in 1994. Here's an eloquent and relevant excerpt:

> Look again at that dot. That's here. That's home. That's us. On it everyone you love, everyone you know, everyone you ever heard of, every human being who ever was, lived out their lives. The aggregate of our joy and suffering, thousands of confident religions, ideologies, and economic doctrines, every hunter and forager, every hero and coward, every creator and destroyer of civilization, every king and peasant, every young couple in love, every mother and father, hopeful child, inventor and explorer, every teacher of morals, every corrupt politician, every "superstar," every "supreme leader," every saint and sinner in the history of our species lived there—on a mote of dust suspended in a sunbeam.[2]

You and I and all of us are inhabitants and stewards of this tiny blue marble. It is our home, our nest, our kin. Here, we breathe its air, drink its water, grow our gardens, do our work, relish in the beauty, comfort and aid each other, explore freedoms, bask in joys, deeply love all the things we've learned to love. All of our pasts are here. Our present is here. If we evolve and we're lucky, our future is here. Everything that's precious, valuable, and beautiful comes from being here. What we create is here for us all.

The disease of outrage that is contagious through social and media channels is a core ill of humanity. It's addictive by design. We are seduced and bamboozled by the addictive-laced designs of social and media channels. Our binary thinking creates debates on the issues that further divide us. These outrage-fueled debates are hypnotizing us into the illusion of our separation. Left versus right. Blue versus red. White versus black. The *haves* versus the *have-nots*. Rich versus poor. Right side of history versus the wrong side. Us versus them. Many of these ideological debates are necessary for truth seeking—the truths that sit behind the debates wait patiently for our attention.

Many of our public debates employ the simplicity of binary thinking, painting the image that issues are simple and two-sided. However, these debates, considerations, and conversations lack the needed nuance to see all sides, all views, all facets in order to land on deeper truths. Most things—issues and opportunities—are not as simple as we seem to want them to be. As a society we tend to lack the presence and patience to hold complex and conflicting conversations.

There are moral high grounds to claim, but they are not binary. And there's something higher to strive for, even attain. The work to do is to ascend beyond the debate and to live in through the influence of the better angels of our core nature, which means allowing not just the goodness of our nature to rise to the top, but the presence in each of us to consider the nuanced complexity of our real issues. Truth with a capital "T" lives here.

The arc of time is, like our universe, long, wide, and expanding. The arc of history bends slowly by our making, our telling, and our shaping. We bend this arc as a universal collective toward the true north of our moral compass. The shaping of this arc is not made only by the rich, the powerful, or the political. What we value bends this arc. We bend it by our actions, our work, our creations, our relations, our protests, our contributions, our successes and failures. It is bent by love. We may barely notice the tiny yet significant acts that add to this collective narrative. We are each contributing the tiny verses in the play of life through each and every story. This is the story of us. Through our work, through our living, through our love, we make the story as we live the story. It is through the daily act of living that we're bending the arc. Each and every one of us bends it in the direction of our values. Because what we value, we live and celebrate. The intentional bending of this arc is our responsibility, if we choose to attend to it.

Many of us won't. Some will remain distracted by the media-fed outrage and urgency that cuts like a blade for our attention. Some will let primal fears and temporal desires lead their attention by running wild through the ever-calling, endless scrolling *feeds* of social media. Some will continue to play the short game, the fear game, the win-at-all cost game, the us versus them game. Some will continue to run a business that mistreats people as disposable resources and depletes the planet. Any one of us can let our ego be seduced by the game where the assumed rules suggest there have to be winners and losers and there's not enough to go around. The unhealthy ego always needs more of everything. It needs competition, it needs gratification, it needs recognition. The ego takes what it can because it is not its job to care for the collective whole—that's the job of the heart. The ego just wants to win the game. In chapter 6, I cover much more about the choices business leaders have in the type of business game played.

But choosing to play this game is completely curable by love. You, dear reader, have a choice in which game you play. Your precious life is there to live any way you wish. As Mary Oliver asks us, "Tell me, what is it you plan to do / With your one wild and precious life?"

Going Further

If you've made it this far, maybe you're willing to go a little further. Perhaps you're seeing the contents of this book as an invitational calling into a way of doing business, a way of playing the game of business with beauty, integrity, belonging, magnetism, and love at its core. I can't promise it will be easy, but easy is overrated. I can't promise it will be beautiful each moment of every day. It won't. Part of beauty is that it's shaped with and by imperfections in its striving to be more beautiful. There's beauty in the striving. You won't always strike a harmonious tone in your work or business. Those around you, even you at times, will feel like you don't belong. You won't always get exactly what you want, but maybe you'll get more than you bargained for.

If you embark on the beautiful business journey, I can promise you an adventure worthy of your precious life. I can promise it will be fulfilling but not easy. I promise that if you choose the path of the beautiful business, you'll be rewarded with a purpose-filled life and business. You'll create a magnetism for your business that will call forward the best of the people within it, and those who, like you, are striving for a more fulfilling way to live and work. I can promise that the investment into shaping a beautiful business will be one that nurtures your own individual growth. You will be better for it. The world will be better for it. You will be more fulfilled in the journey of it. You will be tested to the core, and your ever-evolving character will rise to each occasion. You will learn to love more deeply, give more freely, share more widely, create more deliberately.

This Time, with Soul

There's so little talk about soul these days. We seem comfortable if we reference James Brown and *soul music*. It's fair game for poets, theologians, and philosophers to consider and discuss the soul. In our places of worship, often quarantined on the sabbath, soul is sometimes considered. But why, I wonder, isn't soul spoken about in everyday life? Does the soul have no place in the modernity of our society? In our work? Is soul given no consideration in our daily lives? Does its inclusion belong in our beliefs? Is there an unspoken taboo around the word *soul* or the mentioning of it? Are we simply too busy to talk about the soul? Or is it that we're so comfortable talking about balance sheets, data reports, discussions of the latest outrageous tweet, or the gossip du jour that there's no space for soul-centric conversations? Why aren't we talking about it, tapping into it, nurturing it, exploring and evolving this very animating force that drives us to love what we love and do what we do?

It's easier to build a website or craft a resume than to shape a spirit. But a website won't shelter you from isolation, comfort the sick, feed the hungry, or heal the environment. You are the only one who has sole custody of your life. Your life, here and now. Your whole life. Not just your commute, your desk, your office, or your computer, but your mind, your heart, your longings, your soul.

These considerations of the soul and our work may seem worlds apart. But are they, really? The founding fathers of the US didn't shy away from the topic. As such, it is *self-evident* that *we are endowed by our creator* with this animating force that literally enlivens our biology, physiology, psychology, and economy.

66 **Which the Laws of Nature and of Nature's God entitle them . . . We hold these truths to be self-evident, that all men are created equal,* that they are endowed by their Creator with certain unalienable Rights, that among these are Life, Liberty and the pursuit of Happiness . . .**

— PREAMBLE TO THE US DECLARATION OF INDEPENDENCE

I believe it is a mistake, if not simply selling ourselves short, to leave *soul* out of our conversations around business. The invisible forces that animate us and bond us are worthy of direct infusion into the discussion and practices of our work. The nature of any manifesto, including the US Declaration of Independence, is to state what one firmly believes, the values that are put forth behind those beliefs, and the actionable intent to manifest them into reality.

---

* While there was a truth to "all men are created equal" at the time of writing the Declaration of Independence, it was not true for women or people of color, including Black and Indigenous people.

My conviction is that if business is worth doing, it's worth doing with heart and soul.

The arc of time and view of humanity is as long as you want to see it. No work is done until the creators say it is. A one-hundred-year vision may seem audacious to some and short to others. How you measure your work, your business, your leadership, and your life is up to you. You get to choose what's important, what's valuable, what's beautiful. You can, if you wish, measure quarter-to-quarter profits, and in addition you can measure your impact—how many lives you change for the better, how much good your products and services do, how much belonging your business creates, how much love you put into your work and the world. You can measure the long arc and deep impact your leadership and business make on the people and planet.

The beautiful business is a way of being that's fiercely pragmatic and aspirational. It's shaped. It's molded. It's forged. All with love. It gains traction over time. It grows roots in healthy soil that bears life-affirming fruit. It's a garden of your making on your little or large plot of soil on this tiny blue marble.

The Beautiful Business /
Principles in Action

What Can You Do?

If you've answered the call of the beautiful business, the path forward is up to you. Here are some guiding principles to bring into being your artful version of a beautiful business.

The Principles of a Beautiful Business

Put purpose to work.

By defining and infusing your self-defined purpose, and baking it into your business, you activate a driving force for good. With your purpose infused and activated in every aspect of your business, you build a foundation that is worthy of your mastery. When a team is unified around a common purpose, they become mutually ignited in their work.

Take agency of your evolution.

Know that your life and business are on an ever-evolving path that orbits your purpose. You and your business will continually evolve in the direction of your purpose if you take joyful responsibility for that journey.

Activate self-awareness.

No business will outevolve its leader's own evolution. The key to heightening the growth of your business is to evolve through self-awareness as a leader. By practicing and improving team and individual self-awareness, you heighten the collective consciousness of a unified team and in turn heighten the prospects of your business.

Cultivate trust and belonging.

When people—employees, customers, partners, and all stakeholders—are bonded together by a fusion of values, they gather into a united front. People who are connected through aligned values create belonging. Belonging builds trust and love.

Allow love to show up in your business.

When we allow love to flourish inside our business, we put heart into what we do, and we are fused by the collective effervescence of our vocational passion. When we love what we do, who we do it with, and why we're doing it, we put more care into the journey and the outcomes.

Activate magnetism.

When a united and ignited team goes about their work, they create magnetism. This magnetism attracts like-minded and like-hearted stakeholders who are attracted to and equally committed to the purpose. Through this magnetism, aligned employees, customers, partners, investors, and community members step forward to belong to the cause. Stakeholders that are integrated through this magnetism bond together in unison, making the business a formidable force for good.

Live and work with soul.

The role of the ego is essential for each of us, but when left unchecked, it can act as a petulant child that always wants its own way. When the ego runs the show, it displaces our humanity. By keeping our ego in check, and infusing soul into our life and business, we minimize the ego's desire for complete attention. The ego knows separation, and the soul knows the truth of its interconnectedness. Where the ego takes, the soul creates. The ego thrives on competition, and the soul thrives on cooperation. The ego wants quantity, while the soul wants quality. When you work and live with soul, you change the game you play in business and life.

Integrate your worlds.

When the leaders of any organization understand the infinite power of the interconnectedness of all things, these leaders tap into a wellspring of wisdom, cooperation, connection, and thus amplification. A beautiful business is an integrated way of working with all the united forces around you and for the good of all things connected to your business.

Work with beauty.

Evolved leaders create integrated teams that are clear and aligned with their beliefs. Integrated teams work in harmony with their beliefs and serve the people connected with the organization. People who are connected through aligned values create belonging, which builds trust and love. Belonging creates bonds that unify around a cause or purpose. When a united and ignited team goes about their work, they become more attractive to those who share their values, which creates magnetism. The felt sense of magnetism that comes from a unified team ignited in a common cause is full-spectrum beauty.

There's nothing more powerful than a united group of souls ignited in a common cause with love at the core.

The Entrepreneur as Maker, Craftsman, Artist

In the act of shaping the beautiful business comes intentional acts of beauty. Here, the business leader is a maker, a craftsman, an artist, and a creator of beauty for the world to enjoy and benefit from. I'd like to invite you to think of building and running a business as an action of creation, just like an artist who makes something valuable, meaningful, and impactful. Throughout this book I'll lean into a variety of metaphors that speak to these creative acts ranging from business leader as artist, maker, or gardener.

I believe business is an act of creation because it is made by humans for humans with the primary intent to positively change the current state of things. And I believe that our primary state as humans is the imaginative acts of creation. These creative acts of business are when we're creating something new that changes a set of someones that we call customers.

Examples of business leaders who fit the mold of maker, artist, or gardener include Steve Jobs and Steve Wozniak, Apple cofounders; Hewlett-Packard founders Bill Hewlett and David Packard; Oprah Winfrey of Harpo Productions; Brené Brown, researcher and author; Sara Treleaven Blakely, founder of Spanx; Marcia Griffin, founder of Home Free USA; Morgan DeBaun, founder and CEO of Blavity Inc.; Richard Branson of Virgin brands; Janice Bryant Howroyd, founder and CEO of Act 1 Group; Robert L. Johnson and Sheila Johnson, founders of BET; Cathy Hughes, founder of Urban One; Julia Hartz, cofounder of Eventbrite; Elon Musk of Tesla and SpaceX; Phil Knight, founder of Nike; Berry Gordy, founder of Motown; Bob Hurley of Hurley; and many others. Many of these businesses were founded in garages, spare bedrooms, studios, and kitchen tables by the people who made, crafted, coded, and experimented with their ideas from the onset. At their heart, many are creators who had a vision and the fortitude to tinker around with it and apply sweat and toil to get their company off the ground.

Business done beautifully is an intentional and ongoing act of beauty, a creation that's intended to move people beyond their current way of seeing, living, and working into a new realm of vast possibility. A beautiful business, in this sense, works with the power of possibilities and moves people into a new and better reality.

My Invitation to You

My friends, this book, and implications for the beautiful business within it, is an invitation for a reclamation. It is intended to be a revolution of our highest values. It is both about the morality of business and the values inherent within the beautiful struggle to create something that has lasting value and makes the world a better place. This is a call to awaken to a world of possibility in business. This is the antidote to disconnection, disintegration, and disengagement. This is a remedy to greed, gluttony, injustice, and pride. Make no mistake: the people of our world need this now. In Western culture, people are voting with their values and wallets and taking to the streets. The people that work within organizations are seeking to belong and contribute to something that matters.

It's when beauty is lacking that we need it the most. As a people, we are drowning in the banal. As a culture, we are sick with the disease of productivity. As a society, we are suffocating in tribalism and materialism. In the business world, there is a deprivation of meaning and connection and therefore we hunger to infuse more belonging and purpose in our work.

I am a strong believer in our innate human nature of goodness. The "better angels of our nature," as Abraham Lincoln put it, will ultimately rise above the ails, ills, and shadows of our society. The long tail of time proves this again and again. There are marrow-deep and primal forces at work within us, propelling a goodness of society, of culture, and of a way of being in and of the world. These forces endow us with powerful creative and productive capacities, which, when engaged, can overcome our current sense of separation and disintegration. Our innate ways of being will constantly strive for the horizons of belonging, cooperation, and love.

This is *precisely* **the time when artists go to work. There is no time for despair, no place for self-pity, no need for silence, no room for fear. We speak, we write, we do language. That is how civilizations heal.**

I know the world is bruised and bleeding, and though it is important not to ignore its pain, it is also critical to refuse to succumb to its malevolence. Like failure, chaos contains information that can lead to knowledge—even wisdom. Like art.

— TONI MORRISON

Working Together

" We shape our self
to fit this world

and by the world
are shaped again.

The visible
and the invisible

working together
in common cause,

to produce
the miraculous.

I am thinking of the way
the intangible air

passed at speed
round a shaped wing

easily
holds our weight.

So may we, in this life
trust

to those elements
we have yet to see

or imagine,
and look for the true

shape of our own self,
by forming it well

to the great
intangibles about us.

— DAVID WHYTE[3]

Take your well-disciplined strengths, stretch them between the two great opposing poles, because inside human beings is where God learns.

— RAINER MARIA RILKE

CHAPTER 2

Why a Beautiful Business?

> **❝ An individual has not started living until he can rise above the narrow confines of his individualistic concerns to the broader concerns of all humanity.**

— DR. MARTIN LUTHER KING, JR.

No one asked me to write a book about the beautiful business, what it means, why it's vital or important. At first, some people I have spoken to about this book and the thinking within it seem a little perplexed by the paradoxical notion of a beautiful business. But as Henry Ford is credited for saying, "If I asked people what they wanted, they'd tell me they wanted a faster horse." History teaches us that true innovation goes beyond the expected.

A beautiful business is for and about people who understand the importance and are seeking a more wholeheartedly integrated way of working. A beautiful business is for and about people who know that good business and leadership is difficult, complex, and filled with paradox.

A beautiful business is a journey of evolution. It's a choice to go beyond the simple, easy, and obvious. It's about investigating and living deeper truths in business. Equally important, it's about discovering your truth. A beautiful business gives form and language to the underlying human complexities of business. The journey toward a beautiful business is about helping you identify and activate the foundations of what matters most to you and your business. It's about activating more of our highest human nature—humanity, service, value creation at its best—in the outcome-driven world of business. The path of a beautiful business is about what I've learned on my journey of realizing vital ways of doing business.

Among the truest parts to our humanity is that we are paradoxical. We have the unique ability to hold multiple simultaneous truths together. We are part primal animal tethered to the natural world and part soul-filled beings animated by unseen forces. We are part cooperative beings that shape the world around us and part imaginative beings that envision a future. We are part dreamer, part maker, part security seeker, part possibility creator.

Because of our abilities of self-awareness and imaginative thinking, we are outcasts from the primal animal world we are still connected to. We create the world around us by our actions and inside us by our beliefs. We need both security from threatening forces and social belonging. We're influenced by the world that we and previous generations have created. And yet we're inextricably connected to the natural world from which we currently draw resources and inspiration. We're making the thing as we're living the thing—whether that's a life, a vocation, or a business.

In our businesses, we bring forward our unique gifts as imaginative and cooperative beings that can bring into fruition our dreams and ambitions. It was our ability to both imagine and cultivate this domain that put a man on the moon.

Because of the unique nature of our humanity, we have the ability to envision and journey upon a path of constant evolution for our business and do so in such a way that cultivates work-life satisfaction, environmental mastery, positive relationships, self-awareness, personal and professional mastery, autonomy, personal and business growth, engagement and belonging, and purpose.

We are capable of the most horrible acts of cruelty and the most beautiful acts of kindness. We get to pick the path we follow, the actions we take, the things we think about. We get to choose what our life means and how we live it. In our businesses, we are called to generate profits while caring for people and the planet; to be disciplined in our expertise and curiously explore innovation; to be courageous yet vulnerable in our own humanity. We are called to lead and be led, love and be loved, create and consume, make and be made, teach and be taught, sell and be sold.

The world we live and work in has few absolutes. In business we can both build a business that produces a profit and creates well-being for the team of people inside and outside the business. We can both create a more secure future and create a business that provides a more meaningful life and world. We can both nurture our bottom line and care for the people that surround our business. We do so in community, connection, and continuation toward a future world of our making for ourselves and with others.

The truth is we're always making—our story, our future, our business, our culture, our imagined possibilities—however we envision them. We make up our minds about what's important and what isn't, and we act with heart to live that meaning.

This book is about the business you have chosen to lead, the one you're in the midst of creating, or the one you're envisioning. This book is about the choices you will make in the shaping of that business. This book is for the leader inside you that's calling yourself to a wider, brighter, and evolving world of business possibilities. This book is about dynamic harmony of leadership. It's about the paradox of work. It's about integrating the opposing poles of how we live, how we work, and how we're made. Within the canvas of this book, a healthy business is a beautiful business. It's an ever-evolving entity that bends toward freedom, responsibility, self-awareness, meaning, commitment, humanistic growth, and harmonic integration rather than predominantly striving for status, outward recognition, and winning at all costs.

This book is a calling to the leader who has found themselves in that place that's "beginning to lead everywhere," as David Whyte writes in his poem "Sometimes":[4]

> . . . you come
> to a place
> whose only task
>
> is to trouble you
> with tiny
> but frightening requests
>
> conceived out of nowhere
> but in this place
> beginning to lead everywhere . . .

Beauty? Really?

Beauty is not the superficial adornment or the window dressing that the *beauty* industry would lead you to believe—it is a revolution of values that are inherited from the better angels of our nature. Beauty, in its truest and purest form, is a felt sense of the value system that sits in the marrow of your soul. It is who you are at your core. This is full-spectrum beauty.

There's a scene in the movie *Dead Poets Society* where the free-thinking teacher John Keating, played by Robin Williams, explains the value of poetry, literature, and beauty to his teen students who are potentially future doctors, lawyers, and business leaders.

> We don't read and write poetry because it's cute. We read and write poetry because we are members of the human race. And the human race is filled with passion. And medicine, law, business, engineering: these are noble pursuits and necessary to sustain life. But poetry, beauty, romance, love: these are what we stay alive *for*. To quote from Whitman: "O me! O life! of the questions of these recurring, / Of the endless trains of the faithless, of cities filled with the foolish . . . / What good amid these, O me, O life? / *Answer.* / That you are here—that life exists and identity, / That the powerful play goes on, and you may contribute a verse." That the powerful play *goes on*, and you may contribute a verse. What will your verse be?[5]

That is what beauty is; it is your verse in the making, still inside you and waiting to emerge. It is the passion and values you harness to create your life and build your business.

Over the last two decades, a frequent question that I've heard in various forms from business leaders is "Why do I work so hard and care so much, just to make a profit?"

Usually this question comes after a particularly difficult time in the trajectory of a business. Times of crisis, evolution, and significant challenge tend to be the times when we question, "What's it all for?" All businesses and business leaders will inevitably face crises. When those dark times come, it's important to have an answer to the question **"Why should anyone care about beauty when business is about results?"**

Beauty is not the tangible, final bottom line of results. It is the deep value within, and it can't be destroyed. Even when your business is in the red or is facing serious challenges to its very existence, the core of beauty is still there. By focusing on that center of beauty now, you build a stronger, more vital organization—the one you were always meant to create because it springs from your values and from something far beyond the results, which shift and change with the tides of the economy.

My Journey Toward Beauty

In 2017, I had a seed of an idea that began as I worked on my book *The Evolved Brand*. I had given my colleague an outline and chapters to read over. One of the early-draft chapters was titled "A Beautiful Business." "Tell me about what you mean by 'a beautiful business,'" my colleague encouraged.

It's an idea I had been thinking about for years and that I would later weave into a TEDx talk. I got a lot of interest in my presentation but also many questions. I heard from business leaders who poured heart and soul into their organizations but hesitated to see themselves as artists or makers creating something beautiful. Yet I feel this is the ingredient and the conversation we're missing in business right now.

This book builds on that work; it is an examination, exploration, and actionable manifesto for how beauty, as its deepest meaning, is potent and valuable in business and for the world. And it just may be the antidote to what the world of business and our society needs now.

When I started this book, I didn't set out to write the book that ultimately revealed itself to me. Those who have endeavored into the empty abyss of a blank page, the formation of a business, or nearly any creative or artistic endeavor know this fundamental truth: the clarity of my *why* reveals itself as I travel the path of experience. The deeper I go into an experience, the clearer the landscape of wisdom becomes. The reason I started a business or took my leadership role was not the same reason I stayed there, hunkered down, moved forward, and reinvented myself multiple times as I ventured on. When I started my first business in 1994, I had a newborn and a new business. My original perception of myself was gone. I was burdened with providership and ownership, and yet I insisted I wasn't going to travel the *sellout* business path.

As this book took shape, I kept coming back to these foundational questions:

- What do I know to be true and valuable about the most successful businesses and their leaders?
- What do I believe about business that is inextricably tethered to who I am and how I live as a leader?
- What do I believe needs to be said, and said now, about the journey of a business and its leaders?

The elegance of the answer surprised me: by living a beautiful life, I have built beautiful outcomes. Evolved leaders create beautiful businesses; and beautiful businesses create exponential outcomes. Said differently, the more evolved a person I am, the more evolved my work and business can become. The more clarity I have about why I live and work the way I do, the more I am able to amplify and accelerate the possibilities that lay ahead for my business and life. The more I instill these driving beliefs within my business, the more I attract people that fuse together to drive exponential results. The clearer I am about the values that drive my business actions, the more I create value for my customers. Clarity and intentionality are the thresholds to exponential outcomes. The clearer any of us is about our motivations and beliefs—what drives us to do the difficult work we do—the more belonging, integrity, and magnetism our businesses contain.

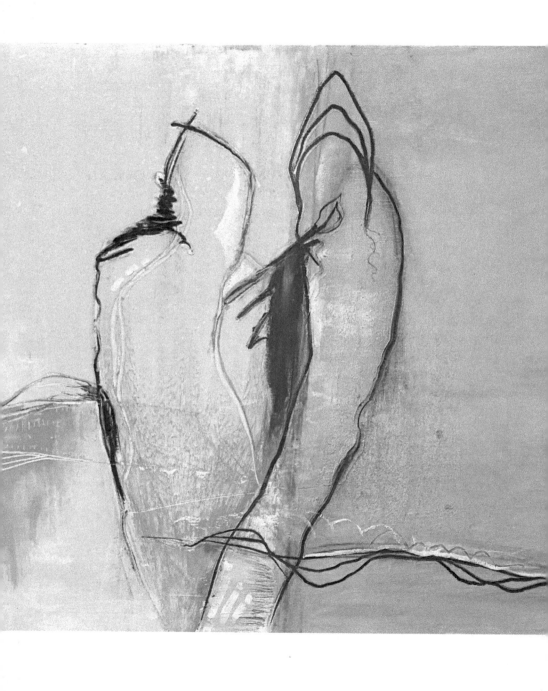

Reclaiming Beauty

The word beauty has been diluted by the cosmetics, entertainment, and fashion industries. The selling of their goods and services would have us believe that beauty is a visually centric attribute that can be fabricated by the adornment of superficial applications all designed to fit an industry-defined mold. Wear these clothes, apply this makeup, cut your hair this way, walk this way, have this body-type, sculpt this chin-line, lip-line, eye-line, and nose-line and you'll be seen as beautiful. It's rubbish. It's one of the biggest lies that the constant drumming of mass media has fed Western society over the last fifty-plus years.

The root of the word beauty comes from the Old French word *beauté*, which connects to the Latin word *bellus*, meaning fine, pleasant, agreeable, or attractive. Beauty, at its core, is the psychological belief of attraction and the spiritual connection of awe. While beauty certainly has physical or visual components, it is ultimately a felt sense that is used to describe something that has the integrity of both inner and outer beauty. Beauty is not something we can simply see but rather is the way something is. Real beauty comes from the center out and you feel it as much as see it. It comes from the core of something that ultimately can be expressed visually.

On April 4, 1967, Dr. Martin Luther King Jr. gave a speech at the Riverside Church in New York City. The title of the speech has been referred to as "Beyond Vietnam."[6] In it, Dr. King referenced what he called the "beautiful struggle." In this speech he states, "Now let us begin. Now let us rededicate ourselves to the long and bitter, but beautiful, struggle for a new world." While his speech was speaking primarily about the civil rights moral revolution to shift us away from an escalating war and the mechanisms that instilled it, it was also a call to shift ourselves away from a "thing-oriented society" to a "person-oriented society." He thereby encouraged and invited us to reclaim the highest, noblest parts of our nature as a way of being.

Beauty is not reserved for special situations, places, businesses, and people. And while it's been explored by some of the greatest thinkers of humankind—from Plato to James Baldwin to Albert Einstein to Joseph Campbell—it does not require deep contemplation. Beauty has its own philosophical study called *aesthetics* and the growing psychological field of *empirical aesthetics* (how people experience beauty and art). But children don't need to be taught how to experience beauty, and it's accessible to anyone, anywhere. It's as common as *love* and can be a way of seeing and moving through the world.

There isn't any single or universal definition of beauty, and it has an inherently subjective nature. In the eye or mind of the beholder, beauty can be defined differently depending on the definer, the viewer, the culture, or the timeframe. In this book I claim a particular definition of beauty, one that frames the experiential world of beauty that is centered on a felt sense that comes from the values woven within our inheritance of the better angels of our nature, our highest and truest selves, rather than a visual depiction.

Consider a Picasso painting, for instance. The artwork is made up of all the components and materials that other artists use—medium, pigment, canvas, brush, training, concept, technique, and composition—all combined to culminate into a whole. A finished piece of art. But the value of the work is not the sum of the components. The material that goes into a Picasso painting might add up to about $400 of supplies but sells for many millions. What's the difference? The art adds heart, soul, and clear intention that creates not just an image but an experience that moves us from one way of experiencing the world to a new way of witnessing the world. This is beauty.

What Is a Beautiful Business?

By a beautiful business, I mean the integrated vital system that stems from the Japanese aesthetic principles of beauty. These defining characteristics include synergy, order, wholeness, gravity, radiance, harmony, and human creation and experience that act in accordance with the laws of nature. This is inside-out beauty that is born from our deepest values. It's an attribute that comes from the DNA of your business, a felt experience with measurable business benefits. It's an attribute that grows from within the organization versus one that is applied to the exterior of the company or brand. When born from and baked-in through the organizational beliefs, beauty becomes a felt sense, an action, and something you experience as much as see.

Far from merely decorative, these attributes create cohesive and sustainable organizations that have their own essential core. This core is the heart and soul of the business. Within this core are the deeply held beliefs of the business leaders that form the intent, values, actions, and expression of the business.

Once the core beliefs and behaviors are defined, implemented, and orchestrated, the beautiful business operates with *integrity*—an integrated system that has its own *magnetism* and creates *belonging* for the people involved. Integrity comes from a genuine wholeness by aligning beliefs and behaviors. Belonging brings people with aligned values wholeheartedly together in a collective and sustained effort. Magnetism attracts like-minded and like-hearted people into and around the beautiful business. When fused together, a beautiful business creates a valuable felt experience that comes from the soul of an integrated business. You feel a beautiful business the way you feel a moment of awe, a beautiful piece of art, a flourishing garden, or a moving experience. The beautiful business is more than the sum of its people, systems, offerings, and various parts.

**66 We ascribe beauty
to that which is
simple; which has no
superfluous parts;
which exactly answers
its end; which stands
related to all things;
which is the mean of
many extremes. It is
the most enduring
quality, and the most
ascending quality.**

— R. W. EMERSON

Beauty by this definition, when applied to business, creates a synergistic whole of integrated parts. Beauty is how you, the awakening business leader, show up in your vocation and life. A beautiful business has integrity, which incorporates an intentional and actionable alignment between its beliefs and behaviors. A beautiful business has a heart and soul that drives for both a healthy bottom line and is altruistic in its approach to serving people. A beautiful business cultivates gravity and creates radiance, order, and harmony. It is regenerative, sustainable, and vital. It is a business that is beautiful inside and out. It is infused with an unignorable integrity that attracts like-minded and like-hearted individuals far and wide.

Beyond Navel-Gazing: Why Beauty Matters

I can practically hear some pragmatists out there quietly ask (or, out loud, groan) the question "Just what's the value of beauty in business?"

In our highly disintegrated society, technology tools have been designed to connect us anywhere. However, some startling statistics are measuring that we're on the road to more loneliness rather than belonging.

In multiple surveys from Stanford University, San Francisco University, Harvard University, William & Mary, Asia Pacific University, Vrije Universiteit Amsterdam, and others that explore social media patterns, it's been identified that people who spend more time using social media daily felt lonelier than those who spent less time using social media. As well, an increase in social media use has been linked with increased distractibility and disturbances in sleep.

I find the studies' language of "use" or "usage" interesting, as it's the same language applied to drug addiction. It's a startling fact that only the drug and social media industries refer to their *customers* as "users." Perhaps this is no accident as many of the biggest social media platforms hire game designers to make their products more addictive.

Former Google design ethicist Tristan Harris, who recently cofounded the Center for Humane Technology, raises the question "Are apps and social media platforms good for you?" Tristan has become one of the most outspoken critics of how devices are intentionally made to addict users at the cost of their time, health, and comfort.

We have some ugly elements to our modernized culture. Today we experience more factions, disintegration, finger-pointing, blaming, and tribalism. We tend to value *things* over *people*, and personal ideology over shared humanity. *Us* versus *them* is at an all-time high. According to social psychologist Jonathan Haidt, "surveys in the United States going back to the 1960s show that we used to slightly dislike the other party and the people in it. But beginning in the 1980s it begins rising, and in the 2000s it rises very quickly, to the point where now members of one party in my country hate the other side so much that many find it deeply offensive even to work in the same office as someone who voted the other way."[7]

In business, too, the drive for output and results creates stress, fear, anxiety, and burnout in cultures that are fear-based and hyperfocused on bottom line. The perceptions created by superficially curated social media feeds are rewarded with likes and clicks. Cultures that value output over impact create psychological landfills—when cultures, in organizations and society, forgo the natural and universal harmony in living and working for the loud, flashy, gaudy, showy, and pretentious.

A beautiful business is valuable because it comes from a leader that intends on building something that creates and holds value beyond profit but includes profit. A garden without a skilled and caring gardener is a meadow. While a meadow may be scenic and things may grow with seed, soil, sun, and rain, you can't harvest a meadow.

As well, you can't create a meaningful piece of art by painting by numbers. The linear processes of business-building that too many MBA programs teach rarely creates exceptionally valuable or beautiful businesses. The works of art by Steve Jobs, Oprah Winfrey, Elon Musk, Tony Hsieh, Ava DuVernay, Phil Knight, Richard Branson, Sara Blakely, Blake Mycoskie, and Yvon Chouinard can't be born by a linear method. Few of these business leaders went to business school or earned an MBA. These are artists-makers that aim their creation through a business venture. They planted their own garden of ideas, primed the soil, tended to their plantings, pruned, fed, and nurtured their ideas into a flourishing garden of business. They forge a movable feast of business that creates a magnetism that their loyalists experience. It's artistry that makes a beautiful business valuable. And while the people I note above may not see themselves as artists, just as you may not see yourself as an artist, you can be one—just by choosing the path of the beautiful business.

> **❝ Beauty was not simply something to behold; it was something one could do.**
>
> — TONI MORRISON, *THE BLUEST EYE*

The Path to Beauty

The act of creation isn't linear. The intention, creation, and refinement process of the artist's way looks more like a spiral of evolution (see visual) than a linear path. When we study how Apple became Apple, or how Patagonia became what it is today, you will discover a series of trials and experimentations that were built on primary beliefs from the business founders that set them off into an exploratory and experimentation process.

The results are that leaders and teams come from slowly forged and refined creations. Creation can be a messy process. It lives frequently in the world of *this might not work*. It's filled with trial and error, fits and starts, experimentation and failure; it's met with the clarity that comes from learning, refinement, and feedback. As Michelangelo has been famously quoted as saying, "In every block of marble I see a statue as plain as though it stood before me, shaped and perfect in attitude and action. I have only to hew away the rough walls that imprison the lovely apparition to reveal it to the other eyes as mine see it."[8]

CHAPTER 3

The Business Evolution

My work has suggested beautiful businesses do not become so overnight. This is good news. You can evolve a beautiful business, no matter where your business is right now. The more challenging truth is that beauty is never finished. The path of a beautiful business and your evolution as a leader is a spiral journey. As you apply your leadership views, you refine your beliefs and thinking. You may come back to the same ideas—creating products, hiring, building teams—more than once, at different levels.

The Evolutionary Curve

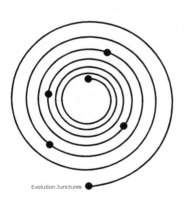

Evolution Junctures

Top View

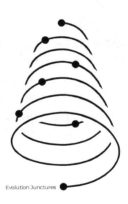

Evolution Junctures

Side View

At the start, you may be thinking of a kinder hiring process. As your company evolves and you reexamine hiring years later, you may realize you have created a soulful culture and will now be hiring based on culture fit. This spiral journey will teach you what you need to know. It may even surprise you in how the journey changes you.

Revealed and earned wisdom is more potent than education simply because it comes from the experience of our unique journey. By walking our own unique path, the path of authenticity, we discover what matters most to us. Through this discovery, we remove obstacles of distraction so we can commit our finite time and attention to what we believe matters. The hard-earned "ahas" in our life will reorient our life trajectory and reframe what we want, what we do, and what we envision is possible.

On the journey to evolving your thinking and approach to a beautiful business, one of the first things you will learn is what matters to you. What is the vision for your beautiful business? What is your true north, your driving purpose, beyond just making money?

Only with the power that comes from committed contemplation can we realize what matters and what doesn't. If we are conscious business leaders, we have likely come to the realization that there's much more to business than just making profit. Of course, making enough money is an essential element that permits us to continue on our business journey. While air, food, water, shelter, and psychological safety are essential for human living, these vital elements are not what we live and work for.

First Steps: Are We Growing or Evolving?

The act of beautiful creation can take many forms. Most business strategists will drive you to create and grow a bigger business, regardless of the size of your current business. Instead of being allowed to nurture our businesses to evolve in greater value and beauty, we're told to aggressively pursue growth. But growth for growth's sake can sometimes be a trap.

Of course, some growth may be needed. A solopreneur may wish to hire at some point to reach more customers. A small business of two hundred employees may want to reach stakeholders in other states or countries by expanding. Publicly traded companies are legally obligated to offer reports on their short-term, quarter-to-quarter profits and to show growth for their shareholders.

But the idea that I need to increase a particular metric at any and all costs can lead to unintended outcomes within a business, such as hiring too fast, onboarding the wrong people, or compromising in quality and innovation. This is not to say that measurement is not important; however, any company can serve a wider set of metrics than simply profit. Companies can measure their innovation output, customer satisfaction and loyalty, or employee trust and engagement, all of which lead to healthy growth.

At the start of my own business, I felt that building profits and growing my business were important to create enough momentum to help many people and to keep my organization open. Of course, this is true. However, as my business grew, I asked myself more about what I was measuring—and why. As such, I began to look at a wider set of metrics that related to the value that my business was creating, and I've helped others do this, too. This internal conversation that I was having regarding the relationship between profit and growth left me reframing a number of questions I was asking:

- What if, instead of growing my business or my influence as fast as possible just to grow, I nurtured their deliberate evolution instead?
- What if, instead of growth for the sake of growth, I thought about how I, my team, and my organization are evolving and what that means for the future of my business and my customers?
- What if, instead of working to sell to more customers, I focused on serving them with greater value?
- What if, instead of driving my business to be bigger for the sake of being bigger, I focused first on getting better and creating more value?

When I thought in terms of evolving (making meaningful change as I adapted to circumstances) and nurturing (protecting something while it grows) instead of rapid growth, I was compelled to be more intentional about *what*, *how*, and *why* I was growing.

If we focus on evolving, we mindfully and creatively adapt to the circumstances that surround us. If we focus on nurturing, we can protect and steward what's already established and valuable. We'll dive more into evolving later in chapter 4, which focuses on what evolution actually is and why it is vital to individuals and leaders alike.

For now, consider these questions:

- In what ways does my business need to grow?
- Can my business serve my customers in ways that are valuable to them and unique to me?
- What type of growth will be most beneficial in helping me and my business thrive?
- How does my business need to evolve internally so it can flourish externally?
- What does healthy, intentional, and sustainable growth look like for me and my team? How would I measure that?
- What are ways I can nurture my team so that they have the direction, focus, and space to engage with one another, serve customers, and innovate?
- How does my leadership, my team, your business, and my brand need to be nurtured?
- What am I unwilling to compromise on to achieve growth? What are the nonnegotiables?

66 **People claim to want to do something that matters, yet they measure themselves against things that don't, and track their progress not in years but in microseconds.**

— RYAN HOLIDAY, *PERENNIAL SELLER: THE ART OF MAKING AND MARKETING WORK THAT LASTS*

Tenets of the Beautiful Business

Through my exploration and study of the key attributes of a beautiful business, I have discovered they boil down to four key tenets: awakened leadership, belonging, magnetism, and integrity. Beautiful businesses can use these tenets as guidelines. When you focus on imbuing your organization with these four principles, you are on the path to building a beautiful business.

The Beautiful Business / Tenets

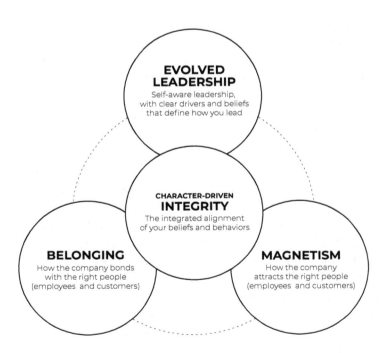

EVOLVED LEADERSHIP
Self-aware leadership, with clear drivers and beliefs that define how you lead

CHARACTER-DRIVEN INTEGRITY
The integrated alignment of your beliefs and behaviors

BELONGING
How the company bonds with the right people (employees and customers)

MAGNETISM
How the company attracts the right people (employees and customers)

Evolved Leadership

No business will ever outevolve its leaders. A business is nothing more than a human-created entity made for other humans. It's made up of rules and structures that we've invented and refined over time. Many of these rules and structures are somewhat arbitrary, and other than legal issues, much should be taken at face value or even challenged. The artist business leader breaks down archaic structures and challenges assumptions—their own and those within conventional systems. All business is for and by people. The business does nothing on its own. So in order for the business to evolve into realizing the key tenets of belonging, integrity, and magnetism, the people—and especially the leaders—in the business need to evolve to a state of readiness.

In Chapter 4: The Evolving Leader, I'll go into more detail on the kind of leadership it takes to run a beautiful business, but for now I'll talk about the courage required to embark upon a beautiful business and leaders' role in that journey.

The world and many workplaces seem hungry for courageous conversations. These are conversations where people are encouraged to respectfully express their views openly and truthfully, without retribution or negative ramification. Out of courageous dialogues, new, deeper, and shared understanding emerges.

It is the leader's job to encourage these conversations at every level of an organization. It takes courage, confidence, trust, faith, and risk. This indeed may be one of the most challenging aspects of leadership, to foster both an environment and an approach for the courageous conversation and to be brave enough to both invite it and listen. Paradoxically, the more courage we bring to our work and work environments, the more openness and trust that exists—thus, more belonging, collaboration, creativity, innovation, and productivity flow.

"Good leadership requires you to surround yourself with people of diverse perspectives who can disagree with you without fear of retaliation.

— DORIS KEARNS GOODWIN

Courage is the degree to which leaders engage in wholehearted participation with life, with others, with community, with work, and with their future. To be evolved is to be self-aware; to know ourselves, our values, our drivers and beliefs, and how our behaviors affect the world around us. To be courageous is to know and plant our values and beliefs deeply in the body, in the culture, and in the world.

Leading ourselves and others with courage is to live up to and into the things that matter most to us, despite their degree of difficulty. To live and work courageously is to stay true to the manner we are made—and how we are made to meet the world.

The best leaders within and among us hold the following together:

- Personal ambition and the good of the whole
- Individual happiness and service to others
- Long-term gains and short-term struggles
- Consistently delivering on promises made to customers and clients with the equally difficult promises made to employees
- The even more difficult promises made to spouses, partners, mates, children, and family
- And the sometimes-impossible promises made to ourselves

The self-aware and courageous leader lives in the intersection of their authentic public profile and more private relationships. Evolved leaders risk the vulnerability to be seen as imperfect—not having all the answers. Leaders are tasked to have a vision, hold that vision, see it through, and nurture a space for their team to thrive. It is this space that leaders inhabit that requires constant courage but also permits great reward.

The difficult dynamic of evolved leadership, emerging or otherwise, is the shift away from the command-and-control system toward a far more dynamic and interrelated way of participating in work. It's a system that demands not only self-belief that allows a leader to speak and have a vision but the vulnerability that enables them to be present to the complex realities of what is and to fully listen. This is the courageous and evolved leadership stance.

> **❝ Vulnerability is not winning or losing; it's having the courage to show up and be seen when we have no control over the outcome. Vulnerability is not weakness; it's our greatest measure of courage.**
>
> — BRENÉ BROWN

Belonging: Creating the Connections That Bond People Together

Harley-Davidson enthusiasts have a near cult-like connection to the brand. From accountants to dentists to rough-riding Hells Angels, the brand attracts a deep sense of connection, regardless of age, demographic, geography, and income status. Harley riders belong to the brand.

This affinity and connection could also be said about Burners, those that have had deep experiences at Burning Man; Googlers, how Google refers to its employees; and Conscious Capitalists, who are people tethered with Conscious Capitalism.

As humans, we're all hard-wired to connect and belong: to people, groups, communities, places, what we do, and ways of life. We do this not only because it creates psychological safety but because we want to become part of something larger than ourselves. When we feel we belong, we also feel safe enough to step outside of our comfort zone, and we then grow and take on new challenges and are free to be ourselves. Belonging allows us to bring our best and most authentic selves to life and work.

And a sense and experience of belonging has never been more important. With the isolation that comes with technology, we are challenged to work in ever-changing business environments, to be productive as a team, to innovate, and to collaborate through remote work while attracting a loyal customer base.

For belonging to be fully expressed in an organizational culture, it should also include justice, equity, diversity, and inclusion (JEDI) or DEI (diversity, equity, and inclusion). Workplace cultures with strong JEDI strategies have been linked to increased organizational productivity, lowered job turnover, and increased innovation.

When we listen and celebrate what is both common and different, we become a wiser, more inclusive, and better organization.

— PAT WADORS

Invisible threads are the strongest ties.

— FRIEDRICH NIETZSCHE

Employees who feel accepted and respected apply their best selves to their work. A 2018 study by *Harvard Business Review* found that organizations with higher-than-average diversity experienced 19 percent higher innovation revenues. This study also cited that the most diverse companies were the most innovative, allowing them to market a greater range of products to consumers.[9]

Brené Brown is well known for talking about the importance of belonging. She notes that there's a big difference, though, between belonging and fitting in. The difference between the two boils down to freedom. "Fitting in," she notes, "is about assessing a situation and becoming who you need to be to be accepted. Belonging, on the other hand, doesn't require us to change who we are; it requires us to be who we are."[10]

In her book *Braving the Wilderness*, Brown asked a group of students to describe the difference between belonging and fitting in. Their answers were insightful:

- "Belonging is being somewhere you want to be, and they want you. Fitting in is being somewhere you really want to be, but they don't care one way or another."
- "Belonging is being accepted for you. Fitting in is being accepted for being like everyone else."
- "I get to be me if I belong. If I have to be like you, I fit in."[11]

Belonging is hard-wired in healthy human experience. Research in neuroscience and psychology shows that our need to belong is a basic human characteristic, and the pain of social exclusion—not belonging—is felt in the same receptors as physical pain. Through inclusion and diversity, we can discover belonging, which in the family of humanity is centered on the integrity between love and our common connection to each other. Belonging is the unifying of many different voices and notes that blend together in the making of a harmony.

There is a through-play between belonging, diversity, and inclusion. An authentic sense of belonging is carried directly into morale, productivity, and effectiveness. When we belong, we are connected through a value system that brings dissimilar people together. Belonging forges a unity regardless of our diversity. We are collectively made more beautiful because of our diversity. Belonging creates a bond of effectiveness from inclusion of people who believe and operate from a common value system. Belonging shapes our behavior because we mimic those in our tribe, which in turn amplifies our common behaviors. We have affinity for the beliefs that bond us, and we have a unity in the manner in which we work. When we talk openly about how we belong, we create the mutual understanding of why we belong.

Belonging forges a common behavior system even when the rules or common values are unstated. When we belong, we pull together in collaboration, unify as a mighty force, and create unlimited exponential outcomes.

> **❝ The hunger to belong is not merely a desire to be attached to something. It is rather sensing that a great transformation and discovery become possible when belonging is sheltered and true. Belonging is a call to integrity and creativity.**
>
> —JOHN O'DONOHUE, *ETERNAL ECHOES*

Belonging is ultimately about mutual commitment: from the employer to the employee, and vice versa; from brand to customer and vice versa; from partner to partner; from stakeholder to stakeholder. When we belong to a community, a team, a brand, or an organization we are tethered by an unseen but fiercely powerful bond. The bond is the common beliefs we hold and what we want to ensure are lived. This seemingly invisible bond shows up in the consistent actions and behaviors that move the business forward and create value for its people.

Integrity: Integrating Your Business into Wholeness

Before I go too deeply into talking about integrity, I'll share a story about harmony and how it relates to integrity. During *The Business Elevation* radio show discussing the topic of the beautiful business, the show host Chris Cooper asked me a question about harmony. He asked, "The human dynamics in the workplace often feels messy and complicated. It seems to me that harmony is when all things are humming along nicely, everyone is getting along, and there is no friction or disharmony. How do you reconcile this?"[12]

Great question. This got me rethinking the role of harmony in a beautiful business. Sometime later I had a conversation with Richard Barrett, founder of Barrett Values Centre, about some of the contents of this book. During this conversation, where I was detailing to him some of my thoughts about belonging, magnetism, and harmony, he suggested that harmony is a subset of integrity and that integrity was really what I was describing as the core tenet. He further commented that "character is a reflection of how you are on the inside, what your intent is, and the level of integrity you display in your relationships." This thinking aligns with my belief that your brand is your character, which I'll explain in more detail in chapter 3.

We know from experience that while harmony is an idealized state where all things are humming along in alignment, much of our work is centered on the difficult, messy, sometimes chaotic human dynamics, which more often yearn for harmony as we go about our work. However, when our internal intentions align with our outward actions, we work in integrity. This is true for individuals, teams, and cultures. So while harmony is often desired in the workplace, when we work with integrity, the alignment between our intentions and our actions allows for both harmony and disharmony.

This radio conversation, and the discussion with Richard Barrett, led me to expand my lens of harmony as a core tenet to the beautiful business. Instead I began to think again of the Japanese aesthetic principles of beauty, which include both harmony and alignment with the laws of nature. When our systems are aligned with the laws of nature, they allow for seasonality, storms, chaos, and sometimes destruction in order to form things anew. And integrity, which is the alignment between beliefs and behaviors, can foster harmony, but it also allows for disharmony.

The question asked live on the air also got me thinking about the stigma associated with the word harmony, which at its core is defined as things that are in accord and agreement in relation to one another. Harmony happens when we have complete commonality. Harmony isn't easy. Harmony requires unity and integrity requires mastery of our integrated wholeness. Integrity calls us to be fully present and to incorporate a wholly aligned way of being. We are most hungry for harmony when things become disharmonious, chaotic, and out-of-order. Also true is that we crave integrity when is it most lacking, especially but not limited to our roles of leadership.

So rather than absolute and constant harmony in the workplace, it's been my experience that integrity is more vital. When what I value and believe is aligned with my actions, I work with a harmonized system of beliefs and behaviors, and I achieve integrity. Integrity can happen only so long as my beliefs are clear and my actions are consistently aligned to those beliefs. Integrity applied to teams is when we know what we're striving for and everyone on my team pulls together in the direction of our striving. When integrity is applied holistically, we can achieve wholeness in our businesses.

Integrity is a character trait in people and companies that communicates a great deal about the values held and how accountable the system is to holding itself to those values. Integrity matters in our professional and personal lives. It is one of those character attributes that conscientious leaders, employees, and customers seek out in their working relationships. Integrity is a nonnegotiable characteristic for leadership. Integrity matters most during these times when so much of the business and leadership world is on display for all to see. Customers seek integrity, recruiters seek integrity, employees seek integrity, and leaders seek integrity in all team members.

Our moral and ethical principles show up in action with integrity and especially reveal themselves when people lack integrity. People and businesses with integrity live by a set of values that transfers into coworker relationships, customer service, and marketing honesty. This fundamental trait in business requires that the individuals and teams are responsible for what they say, what they do, how they behave, and how they hold others accountable for the same.

There is a well-known tool that some business cultures and agile teams use called the "say:do" ratio. It essentially measures the proportion of times people follow through on their word. If they say they'll do a certain task by a certain time, it's the likelihood that they'll consistently deliver on it. A high say:do ratio, perhaps even a 1:1 ratio, meaning that person is 100 percent reliable, builds trust and fidelity. Being impeccable with our word, as a business or an individual, is ultimately what builds trust and integrity within our team. When we can count on one another, and our employees and customers can count on us to consistently deliver on our word or our promise to them, we will gain trust and create integrity.

❝ I define integrity as honoring your word. A person with integrity keeps her promises whenever possible, and still honors them if she is unable to do so. You make a grounded promise by committing only to deliver what you believe you can deliver. You keep the promise by delivering it. And you can still honor the promise when you can't keep it by letting the person you are promising know of the situation, and taking care of the consequences.

— FRED KOFMAN, *THE MEANING REVOLUTION: THE POWER OF TRANSCENDENT LEADERSHIP*

Magnetism: Resonance That Creates Unignorable Attraction

I'm at a Super Bowl party hanging out with a group of friends and neighbors and watching both the game and the commercials. A light beer commercial plays with a quirky saying that the actors are repeating over and over, drilling it into the unsuspecting minds of the viewers. One of my friends turns to me and says, "I don't get it. If that's branding, I don't understand why they're spending millions of dollars on a ridiculous saying."

I quickly quip, "Oh no, that's not branding. That's advertising. They're preying on the subconscious of the common-denominator viewer, trying to distract our attention and make us remember their brand name with the hope that next time we need a cheap beer, we think of theirs."

The reason companies spend millions of dollars for a big ad spot is so more people will know about their products or services. Conventional wisdom would seem to dictate that if more people know about your products or services, then you'll be more successful in sales. But here's the rub: more people knowing about your products or services doesn't necessarily convert more customers. Further reach and more awareness doesn't make your company, products, or services any better—just better known.

Alongside recognition, brands would be wise to seek *resonance*, which creates magnetism. As we know, like attracts like.

One of the ways people tend to define beauty is to say that beauty can be subjective. What Harley-Davidson fans find beautiful is likely different than what Subaru, Nike, or Patagonia buyers find beautiful. What resonates with you likely differs from what resonates with your neighbor.

Magnetism happens when like attracts like. A brand's most valuable customers are those that respond to what it does best. This is resonance.

When you focus on resonating with your audience, you shift toward serving the right people in the right way—in a manner that's true for you and valuable to them. In creating magnetism and resonance, brands stop chasing customers and turn to a more powerful force: attraction. Here the brand acts as the flame that burns bright with attraction and not the moth that's chasing the light.

Magnetism is the measured connection of a brand's meanings within the contexts of the people that are connected to the organization. Customers, employees, partners, and investors—all business stakeholders—can all be pulled by the magnetism of a brand.

Here's an example: when I take a Lyft or Uber ride, I'm directly connecting with an ecosystem of shared ridership, and I then have direct magnetism with the drivers and therefore the rideshare system.

A brand can build magnetism through three routes:

1. **Personal Magnetism** is the alignment between a brand's claimed position and meaning, and how that fits within the consumer's life. A Patagonia customer, for example, may be someone who experiences the freedom and expression of immersing in the silent sports that the brand supports. These customers are magnetically drawn to the brand because of their shared values and experiences.

2. **Cultural Magnetism** measures the degree to which a brand's intended beliefs and meanings mirror, reinforce, echo, and reshape the meanings from the social space that consumers inhabit or access in defining and shaping their lives. These may include brands that represent a core cultural value. An example of this is how the Boston Red Sox create a historical magnetism with their fans. Or how Nike invites customer athletes to embrace a "just do it" mindset that connects with Bo Jackson, Michael Jordan, and Tiger Woods, who've each lived out "just do it" in the spotlight.

3. **Organizational Magnetism** refers to the orientation of the brand's designed meanings within the broader systems, structures, and behaviors of the organization. This creates magnetism on a systematic level and creates shared understanding and belonging from the employee level. This type of magnetism is business-model thinking. One business I work with designates *storytellers* to share the pinnacle historical stories with organizational attributes that makes their 110-year-old company unique. All stories that are captured and shared connect to the core values of the organization, which brings them to life in real time, even though the story might be from years or decades ago. Team members from throughout the organization know and share the historical stories and associated core values. When new employees are hired onto the team, the stories and values are interconnected, bringing both to life.

In order to achieve magnetism on any level, your brand needs to be clear about what it stands for, who it is, and who it is not. Your brand must address what its customer wants and needs in a way that customers not only understand but can also emotionally respond to. Creating magnetism begins with aligning beliefs—your brand's and your customers'. It continues as your brand serves the needs of its customers in a way that's true to who it is.

Brand stories, wherever they show up, resonate when brand leaders focus on finding their tribe. Wise brands persistently pursue the trifecta of self-awareness (individual and organizational), customer awareness, and market awareness. I'll talk more about self-awareness in chapter 5.

It's worth a reminder that we don't buy from brands because of what they make or do. We buy from them because of what they *represent* through the *promise* that brands offer and consistently fulfill.

Beauty Takes Aim

As you consider the four tenets of a beautiful business and explore how you might apply them, you will likely notice how you approach them will depend on who you are building your business for. Before you can shape and apply evolved leadership, belonging, integrity, and magnetism, you need to know who you're building your business for.

There's no such thing as a company that's built for everybody. Even the largest companies on earth are not for everybody. Amazon, for instance, can only reach people with reliable internet and an address to deliver goods to. This cuts out 30 percent or more of the world's population. In Western culture—in the US, for instance— even a huge company like Walmart is not for everybody— it's for anyone who wants inexpensive, mass produced goods. Also true is that mass media is becoming more and more of a myth. With the advent of social media, mass media is now segmented into microaudiences called tribes. Seth Godin is well known for his views and writings in his multiple books, including *Tribes*.

A tribe is essentially a group of people who have a common value set in common. Seth Godin talked about it this way in his OnBeing interview with Krista Tippet:

> In the desert or the jungle, the tribe was defined by geography alone. You were in the tribe based on where you were born. Then if we fast-forward to, I don't know, Mark Twain. Mark Twain would show up in a city and a thousand people would come to hear him speak. And everyone who came was in his tribe. They were in the tribe of slightly satirical, slightly jaundiced people who were also intellectuals who could engage with him.

And he had never met them before, but within minutes, they were part of a congruent group who understood each other. So if we fast-forward to today you can take someone who hangs out in the East Village or Manhattan who has twenty-seven tattoos—they go to Amsterdam, they can find someone in Amsterdam who talks their language and acts like them, because they've chosen the same set of things that excite them and that they believe in. And we divide tribes as small a group as we want. But what the internet has done is meant that we don't have to get on a plane anymore to meet strangers who are like us.[13]

You're going after the wrong metric if your business tries to attract everybody. Knowing who you're looking to create belonging, harmony, and magnetism with is critical. Knowing this can define your tribe. Again, Seth Godin shares a perspective from the famous stock investor Ben Graham, which points out that the market, in the beginning, is a voting machine. The focus is to see how many people you can attract to vote for you and raise their voice to say, "I like that." However, in the long game, the market is a weighing machine. Here the market turns into a scale that measures how much impact you have. Those who play and win this game are focused on long-term impact. Again, you won't impact everyone, so knowing just who and how you're impacting them can affect both the voting and weighing machines. As Godin points out, for some brands all you really need is one thousand loyal fans to fan the flames of your business.

One side note: there is a danger in tribalism. Some of what defines tribalism is what we're experiencing in certain parts of our culture now, especially political and social divides. The tribalists mentality has a good deal to do with spotlighting how others are different than us. When this is taken to far extremes, it can lead to disintegration and the "us versus them" mindset. This isn't healthy for brands or people.

There is no end to the good you can do if you don't care who gets the credit.

— COLIN POWELL

CHAPTER 5

The Evolving Leader

Who Is an Evolving Leader?

You know who you are. You either consciously know or you have the intuitive inclination that there can be more in business beyond counting coins and running up the score. It's highly likely that if you picked this book up or someone shared this book with you, you're either an evolved leader or on the road to getting there.

How can you know you're an evolving leader—or at least heading on that journey? How can you orient yourself and know where you are on your leadership journey?

Regardless of what got you here, this evolving path is often not a singular event but often looks more like an unfolding—a slow gestation that reveals its beauty over time. The simplest way that I can express this unfolding is the career path that goes from "I'm not very important" to "I am important" to "I want to do important work."

During my "I'm unimportant" stage,
I was working on the skills of my craft
until I reached a certain level of mastery.
Here I had the confidence to grow into
the "I am important" stage. As a leader,
I then realized that my mastery applied
to purposeless outcomes was mostly
a futile waste of energy, so I evolved to
the commitment of "doing important
work" of transcendent value. Here, I work
to apply my entire suite of mastery
to things of significance. Ultimately,
evolving leaders use the alchemy of their
mastery to transform the world.

Recognizing the Evolving Leader

From time to time, I've had the honor to encounter people who radiate something very special from their center. These individuals have a light within them that shines unignorably bright. They seem to know who they are and why they are here. They move through the world with a wholeheartedness in their relationships, experiences, and vocation. They radiate equal parts joy and focus and have a clear sense of their relationship with themselves and the world. They have made commitments in all aspects of their lives from the clarity that comes from their deeply held beliefs. They live based on these commitments. Their most pressing decisions and even day-to-day rituals are designed to serve these commitments. They are whole and have integrity.

These individuals tend to be unshakable. Their beliefs are applied through the practices that surround their days. They tend to be kind and generous. They are humble yet confident. They are curious, sometimes skeptical, and have mastered the art of deep listening. They are joyful in the immersions of experiences that might seem mundane but are rich with meaning. What might appear as play to others is work to them. And they're constantly working on self-improvement.

These rare people are far from perfect. Just like everyone, they get stressed, annoyed, and tired. They are not immune to and do not ignore the harsh realities that confront the human experience. However, they tend to be constantly noticing and evaluating themselves and the situations around them, especially with an eye to possibilities. They seem to have a high degree of self-awareness, which includes an understanding of their internal self, including their values, and how others see them. They are aware of their effects on people and their impact as leaders.

Most of the time they can see the difference between deep truths and smoke-and-mirror lies. They tend to focus on the big picture and long view, and they can sort out the urgent from the important. They tend to be more interested in what's possible than the facts that define the past without ignoring history lessons. They live and work with a sense of agency. They seem to be living beyond their ego and are oriented to a higher calling. And though they may not openly offer it, their focused intent often falls into the realms of service to some greater good.

When asked, they have likely experienced some sort of awakening or turning point. They may have been confronted with a serious life circumstance—death, divorce, disaster, or some version of failure—and emerged more committed and more lucid in their knowing of why they are here and what they will do with their life. Or perhaps they've traveled a contemplative path of deep processing and introspection that comes from the reflection of their life experiences. Their life has meaning, and that meaning is their compass. They have come to the realization that there's more to living, working, and leading than just making a good or great living, and they are likely to be making a good living and living a good life because of this realization. Or some have hit it big in business and look around at the scenery of their success and ask, "Is this really all there is?"

Perhaps This Is You?

By *leader* I don't necessarily mean the CEO or company president of a company or division manager. A *leader* can be anyone at any level in any organization. For instance, you can be an *intrapreneur*—a change-making someone who works within the boundaries of an organization that has seized the opportunity to change for the better that which you can affect. This change might affect just a small team of people that works within a larger structure, or an entire division to a global organization. Regardless, if you're taking up the charge to make change, you're a leader. The only criteria to be a *leader* is to have authority and agency to change things—to create something out of seemingly nothing by imagination, hard work, and purpose.

Your leadership domain could be the project that sits on your desk today, the team that you're managing to market products, your solopreneurship side-hustle, or the company you're in charge of navigating into the future. In aboriginal cultures in Australia, it is common practice for anyone in the tribe, from the youngest to the oldest members, to lead the walkabout on any given day. In wolf packs, too, the alpha male and female tend to be at the back of the pack allowing others to lead and set the pace.

Leadership is defined more by mindset of responsibility than by title, role, or years of experience. Leadership sees what's possible and aligns the mastered or practiced kit of parts and manageable forces to make it happen. Evolving leaders are alchemists of possibility.

Attending Our Calling to Evolve

Those who exude this radiant light apply the fruits of their evolution to all aspects of their lives, including their vocation. Your vocational path is a disguise as your own individual evolution. In a way, this book is both for and about us, the evolving business leaders. This book is called an "actionable manifesto" because it's not just a declaration of what leaders of a beautiful business might believe, but it's also for those leaders to manifest these beliefs into action—to activate and realize the outcomes of these beliefs. Beliefs are not enough. Action born from those beliefs is what becomes manifest.

This urging to go beyond business as usual may feel like an itch that needs scratching. Or it could feel like a sense of uneasiness on your current path—an unarticulated nudging that sits just below the surface of your conscious awareness, taking us to the edge of your comfort zone and sometimes beyond. It can ignite suddenly as an inferno in your belly—an unignorable rumbling that comes from nowhere but begins to lead anywhere.

You either know it outright or have a sense that your business, regardless of size and scale, can be a beautiful force worthy of the challenges you face day in and day out. You are being summoned to answer the call to create your life and business, so it becomes a rejuvenating force for good—a system of service that makes a positive impact on the world. This includes the industry your business is included within and the people it serves and beyond. And you know that you can make money while making an impact. All good business is sustainable business that thrives to see another day, year, or decade. All businesses require profit or enoughness in a nonprofit venture in order to continue and innovate into the future.

Like anything we give our attention to, it becomes more coherent and actionable when we closely examine it. Our attention, like our time on this planet, is finite. What we give our attention to is where we'll see outcomes. What we feed, water, and nurture will grow and flourish. This attention-giving is where personal evolution and the leadership domain lives. This unfolding makes leaders both students and creators of the life trajectory you deliberately choose to pursue. We nurture ourselves by being aware of ourselves. We do this by deliberately choosing which seeds to plant, which weeds to pull, and which soil to fertilize, and by attending to what needs watering and when it needs water. This type of self-nourishment goes beyond the statistical mentality and works with invisibles that include intuition, beliefs, and ideas. Here the leader becomes both the gardener and the garden; the coach, trainer, and player; the writer, director, and actor.

By knowing that your business begins with the invisibles of beliefs and ideas, by actively inhabiting those invisibles, by filling these invisibles with integrated behaviors, the beauty of the business comes to life. In doing so, the business becomes steeped in a vital life force, your life force. Living the business gives rise to your belonging to it, and gives rise and belonging to others who are connected to it. By inhabiting the business with this life force, it creates a magnetism. By integrating the invisible beliefs and ideas throughout the business, harmony ensues.

I'll let you in on a secret and dispel a myth. All work is personal. The myth of checking one's self at the door of the office has never been doable. Companies have tried this request and failed. All people bring their whole self to their work. When your work is aligned with your calling, your best self shows up in your work. The vocational path, the leadership path, is simply a disguise for the individual, personal, and, for some, even a spiritual evolution. No business will outevolve its leaders. No business will outgrow the leaders' own capacity. And no business will be smaller than the leaders' own evolution. In order for the business to grow and flourish, the leader must evolve.

What man actually needs is not a tensionless state but rather the striving and struggling for a worthwhile goal.

— VIKTOR FRANKL

What Brings Me Here

To give you a sense of how evolution can happen at any stage of leadership, a bit of my personal history may help. As far back as I can remember, I've been obsessed with the elements that lay at the foundation of *The Beautiful Business*.

As a kid, growing up in the lower-middle-class suburbs of Wilmington, Delaware, as often as not, you'd see me with pencil and paper drawing what I saw and what I imagined. Part of this was the practice of noticing and capturing what I appreciated. Some of this practice was simply exploring how to express my rich inner world. And another part was a self-preservation practice as a highly introverted kid.

In the fourth or fifth grade, I had an art teacher named Mr. Bartoli. I still remember the smell of plaster dust, charcoal, and acrylic paint. The high four-legged grey metal stools were the only way to access the high wooden studio work benches. The walls of the art room were filled with student artwork and prints of Picasso, Van Gogh, Rembrandt, and other artists I didn't know. There was a seemingly endless supply of any art material imaginable: paints, brushes, clay, plaster, canvas, paper of all shapes and sizes. The art room was completely different from every other classroom. It was a sanctuary. And I loved it.

One day Mr. Bartoli pulled me aside at the end of class. Prior to that, I had only been pulled aside when I was in trouble for something. As my fellow students collected their belongings and began to file out of class, I had a lump in my throat. He began to talk to me about one of the pieces I had created. But, instead of being in trouble for something, he spoke in a kind and generous tone, complimenting my work. "Your artwork, Steve, has such great detail," I recall him pointing out. "I can see how you focus yourself during class. You clearly understand how to create beautiful things that are unique to you. You put so much care into your art, and it shows."

The following week was parent-teacher conferences. For elementary school kids like myself, it was an uncomfortable ritual to be with your parents in the halls of your school and be paraded from classroom to classroom, teacher to teacher to talk about you and your schooling. I remember being the subject of these parent-teacher conversations but not part of the conversations, until we got to the art room. As Mr. Bartoli spoke to my parents, he echoed what he shared with me. And then he went further. "You know, Steve puts such care in his artwork, as you can see," as he referenced various pieces, "that I think he may have a future in the arts."

What didn't dawn on me until many years later is that Mr. Bartoli's encouragement began to shape part of my identity.

What I didn't know that I now realize is that much of creativity is about deep noticing and pulling together uncommon things in reimagined ways. Because of my introverted nature, the fact that I'm a middle child, and the sometimes-combustible nature of my family environment, I tend to hover quietly below the radar and give special notice to the wide ranges of interactions, emotions, sensations, relationships, and connections people make or attempt to make in my world. In this quieted world, I study people. I closely examine what they're doing, assess why they're doing it, and notice how people relate to one another. I have always been deeply fascinated by how people, who seem so different, manage to cohabitate, relate, communicate, and find common ground. This fascination extends to the subtle things sitting below the surface of obvious behaviors, such as their motivations, fears, wants, needs, and dreams. I've spent a fair bit of my life living in the hearts and heads of other people.

My parents, for instance, couldn't be more different from one another. And the ongoing friction showed at home. My mom was raised in an Irish-Catholic home, filled with rich rituals and guilt-ridden teachings. Along with her four siblings, she attended precocial school through high school and, as a result, our family, aside from my dad, were run-of-the-mill *Cathoholics*. Despite or maybe because of that restrained upbringing, she has a free-spirit streak and was encouraging of my creative outlets. Many of my mom's male relatives—my uncles and great uncles—served in the military, mostly the Navy and Army, and were avid outdoor sportsmen, including hunting and fishing. Just as many of them were part hippies and part hunters. An unusual pairing to be sure. They shot at, killed, and ate nearly everything that squawked, quacked, grunted, honked, chirped, or didn't make a sound. Spitting out lead buckshot while eating Christmas goose gives me mixed-feeling memories. These uncles, along with my mom and aunts, turned me on to some of the best of the '60s and '70s classic and folk rock as it was released on vinyl, which encouraged my appreciation for the counterculture movement that I was far too young to understand at the time.

My dad, on the other hand, was brought up in a strict conservative half-Protestant, half-Catholic household with a puritan and craftsman work ethic. There are still pieces of hand-made wood furniture in my family that were made by my great-grandfather, who was a wood craftsman by trade. My paternal grandfather was overbearingly strict, according to my dad. He wouldn't allow my grandmother to go to Catholic church, work out of the house, or drive. He was a scandalous nineteen years older than his wife, my grandmother, and was aging into dementia by the time I was old enough to be aware of him. When my own father was seventeen, he taught his mom to drive without my grandfather's approval or knowing. My dad's side of the family was focused on a service-oriented mindset, whose primary outlet for service was the Brandywine 100 Volunteer Firehouse in the Elsmere community of Wilmington. My dad, grandmother, aunt, cousins, great uncles, and beyond served as volunteers in this firehouse, accumulating well over one hundred years of service. My grandmother and aunt, along with other female relatives and nonrelatives, served on the Ladies Auxiliary, which buoyed everything that wasn't on fire. This essentially meant these women ran the show, which, if you knew my grandmother and aunt, wouldn't surprise you at all. I have many memories of Christmas parties, weddings, and funerals at the firehall, and as a kid, my brothers and I were mostly permitted to climb the parked fire trucks that smelled of smoke and diesel and try on the heavy fireman metal helmets and thick leather jackets and huge rubber boots. This was, of course, a wonderland for a young boy.

The service-oriented work ethic of my family got me working relatively young. One of my first jobs was when I had a newspaper route starting at the age of eleven. My older brother and I shared delivering the morning *News Journal* to two neighborhoods—about seventy-five houses total. When my older brother retired from the route, I kept it with my younger brother—the plight of the middle child. It was hard work. Every day of the year, we rose at five a.m. to go out into whatever the weather had brought and fold, rubber-band, bag, and then deliver the papers. Rain, snow, dark, Christmas, my birthday, every day, no matter what—I delivered the paper.

On my paper route I saw, more or less, the same faces and places. Some folks were early risers, waiting for their paper in their bathrobe with a cup of coffee in hand at their doorsteps. Others were out for an early walk with their dog. Mostly, though, it was solitary work where I didn't see or talk to anyone.

Upon reflection, I learned to love the quietude of the early morning. And, in hindsight, I loved both creating my own morning rituals and being part of the morning rituals of the families on my route. I remember thinking many times that the news of the day being brought to their doorstep was an honor for me. I was, in a way, bringing them a window to their world. It was a privilege to be part of their daily rituals and welcome them into their day.

To be honest, I didn't always love it. Riding my bike in the predawn dark on a snowy or rain-soaked morning with a third of my skinny-frame body weight of newspapers balanced on the bike frame or slung over my shoulder wasn't easy. But on those difficult days, I tried to remind myself how important the news was to them. This was the preinternet days of the 1970s. The paper I brought was part of their morning ritual and a window into the world and local events. And therefore I was part of their morning ritual. My brothers and I got to know everyone on our route, especially when it came to money collection time. Once a month we went house-to-house to collect next month's paper delivery cost.

Some families were more welcoming and appreciative than others. One man on our route was a World War II veteran who survived Pearl Harbor. We hung on the stories he told, which he did happily and frequently. Some were generous tippers, especially around the holidays. Some would mostly complain about a day when a paper was wet due to the rain or something else. One family's dog was notorious for eating the paper when I slid it through their mail slot, which, to this family, I was responsible for. I didn't have a clue how to fix that.

How we prepared and delivered the paper mattered to them. It was the little things. We had to protect the papers from the rain and wind, be there on time, every day. The more we focused on getting the little things right, the more their rituals served them. If the paper was late or wet, their ritual was thrown off.

Because I had a paper route, it also meant that I had a bike. A bike equates to freedom to a ten-year-old boy, especially in a time when I could head out on a summer's day and do pretty much anything I wanted, so long as my chores were done, and I was home for dinner. And because we lived on the edge of a developing suburb, there were farms and wilderness nearby. More times than I could count, I'd find myself exploring woodlands, trout and bass fishing in some pond or stream, horseback riding at a local stable, or trespassing in a farmer's corn or soybean field. Nature and farms captured my imagination. I've always felt bonded to the creative elements of nature and a home in the wilderness. And perhaps this is why I still love trail running, surfing, and hiking.

When it came time to go to college, I chose a school where I could study fine arts—painting to be precise— and where I could explore studies in the humanities, including psychology, philosophy, and sociology. This combination of artistic storytelling and expression, fused with the deep study of what drives us, motivates us, and makes us tick as humans, has been under the feet of my life path ever since.

As I moved through my undergraduate work, I discovered the world of design and communication, through a summer internship in Marblehead, MA, on the north shore of Boston. During this internship, I was enamored with the way ideas were expressed verbally and visually in order to represent business ideas and offerings. As I set my sights on graduate school, I applied to both fine art painting programs and design programs. I figured I'd leave it up to fate. First, I'd apply to my top-choice schools and see where I was accepted. Second, I'd see if I could earn a scholarship or assistantship because I was paying my own way. The latter panned out for me with an assistantship at Tyler School of Art, Temple University, where I earned an MFA in design and was also allowed to take graduate-level painting courses with the well-known painting dean Margo Margolis. While I've never stopped painting, I set off on my educational then vocational journey as a designer.

As an artist and designer, I'm trained in the creation of things that move people emotionally and intellectually—the creation of beautiful things. As I previously noted, I've had the honor to work with the poet-philosopher David Whyte in his Invitas program on conversational leadership, which widened my view of how leaders can tether their individual growth with deeper wholeheartedness. I also have a minor in psychology, with a focus on the works of Carl Jung and Abraham Maslow. This includes Maslow's Hierarchy of Human Needs and a particular fascination with Jung's work on *Archetypes and the Collective Unconscious*, *Man and His Symbols*, and *Modern Man in Search of the Soul*. Jung's work led me to Joseph Campbell. And I've delved deeply into countless works by Joseph Campbell's mythology mapping, symbolism, and the hero's journey, based on Jung's work.

As well, I've been working as an entrepreneur and business leader since 1994. My business training is primarily through my experiences of starting, building, and running my own company for twenty-three years and working with companies, including Sony, Samsung, Habitat for Humanity, Amazon, the Robert Wood Johnson Foundation, the NFL and MLB, Hasbro, Mattel, ESPN, the Medill School of Journalism at Northwestern University, and many more. I've calculated that I've had the honor to work with more than three thousand business leaders at more than two hundred fifty companies and counting. In essence, I've been working on mastering and bringing my business artistry to work my entire life. And my journey continues with the humble attitude that the more I learn, the less I know.

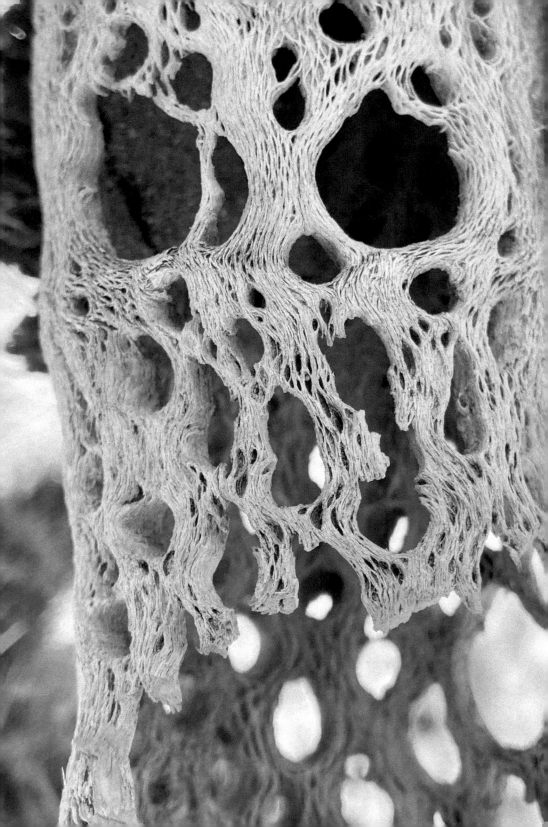

While my position as a business leader started in 1994, the seeds of my evolution started much earlier. My childhood prepared me with a service mindset, a strong work ethic and motivation to create, and a deep connection to the natural world. Of course, it's only in hindsight that I'm able to see the unique journey of my own evolution.

The reflective hindsight of my own evolution weaves a clearer tapestry of how I evolved to who I am now. I wish I could point to a linear path that would indicate this plus this equals that. But life doesn't unfold that way. While our biographical timeline may seem linear, our own evolution isn't. We spiral around our beliefs and callings, sometimes misstepping, choosing things that distract us, or simply experimenting. And, of course, the unpredictability of life unfolds. I don't really know how I evolved from this to that, but I have a sense that the bridges within my journey are a beautifully imperfect, woven tapestry of my own evolution.

These unique ingredients led me to the beautiful business. Your own journey includes the elements you need for your own path to a beautiful business.

A Tale of Two Teams

Monday, Three p.m.

I was leading a presentation with a prominent financial institution to present research findings and brand directions. This company handled a lot of other people's money with a good deal at stake and a national presence. My presentation was to the executive team overseeing the company's marketing committee. The strategies that I was presenting were the translations of a brand and culture process that had been approved by the company's VP of marketing, who was the chairperson of the marketing committee.

As part of my typical process, I employed a mix of qualitative and quantitative research to gain insight into the brand perceptions. In this case, the client had insisted they would be doing that research internally, due to what they cited as time and budget constraints. I gave the client the list information that would be required for benchmarking. The client deployed the research and afterward shared their insight perspectives. Building on their insights mined from this information, my team and I created a brand vision document in collaboration with the client. In short, I entrusted the client to do the collective homework and research, and they were coauthors in the process. Key objectives were defined by the client, which informed the strategic direction of the work at hand.

The meeting started, and I had my presentation ready. Introductions were made by the chairperson of the twelve-member group. When it was my turn to go, I launched into my presentation. Not one full minute into the presentation, and a murmur began to rise from the room. At this stage I was not even one-tenth of my way through what I had to say, and I was cut off. Voices spoke on top of one another. A stress-filled sound collision happened. Comments were tossed about like a hot potato. I was in the eye of a hurricane. In a very short time, I realized that no one was in control of the meeting. I felt like I had been thrown into a washing machine, full speed—rinse cycle.

What I wanted to do was head for the nearest exit as fast as possible. Instead, after a few minutes of the chaos in the room, I chimed in, "Can we go around the room, one at a time, and voice our thoughts and feelings about what's being seen, felt, and heard here?"

In reluctant agreement, one by one, each person voiced their perspective in a way that could be ingested and understood, still not without regular interruption by others. Each member of this leadership group had to fight to have their thoughts and feelings heard. Some perspectives were constructive, others were self-serving, combative, or worse. In the end, I realized I had been thrown under the bus by the leader in charge of the project, and it was moving at about one hundred miles per hour.

The inner chaos of this organization was so deep that the VP of marketing had not fully included any others in her decision to shift such dramatic brand and culture changes, and she used me and my team as the scapegoat to press her agenda and test her intentions. The group was not in consensus as to who they were and what their brand stood for. They had big problems, and because of this, so did I. Not only had I stuck my neck out there to present, but I was not supported when it came time to explain why we had taken this direction. I left the meeting feeling like I had failed, which was true, even though I had based the direction on client-driven information.

Next Week: Tuesday, Twelve Noon

Traveling to the East Coast, I was scheduled to present a findings and recommendations report during a leadership offsite at another financial company. This was a different kind of organization that also happened to handle a lot of other people's money with a great deal at stake and a national presence. By contrast, my team and I handled the four-month research process, which fused qualitative and quantitative investigation and included a wide array of organizational stakeholders and external audience member perspectives. The data was collected and culled, and I developed insights and recommendations to share with the leadership team. Similar to the Monday client, this also called for dramatic shifts in the organization's brand and position in the marketplace.

My presentation was the only item on the lunch meeting agenda. I began to have flashbacks of the previous Monday's presentation. Before I could create a distraction and run, I cleared my head, took a deep breath, and launched into my presentation. I walked through the research process, shared the candid feedback, and distilled it into key findings and related recommendations. After I got through all of what I was there to present, I opened the floor for questions and thoughts. Politely, one by one, the committee members expressed their questions and stated their feelings. No one interrupted. No one talked on top of another. People even raised their hands to be heard next. The discussion lasted for forty-five minutes. Dramatic shifts were agreed to, just like at the Monday's client meeting, but this leadership team took all the information in and assessed, as a unified team, what to do with it. It was clear that in the time given for the meeting and the importance of the work's impact, further exploration and discussion was necessary. I suggested a series of follow-up strategy sessions with the leadership team to better assess next steps and final implementation. All of this was agreed to.

Contrasts in Leadership

I heard it or read it more times than I can count from more sources than I can cite: our approach influences our outcomes. In the two very real situations shared above, there was a stark contrast in approach. The leadership styles—the manner in which they made decisions and led the team—had a great deal to do with the outcomes, which, in turn, showed up in the way each culture behaved, and ultimately in the results. The Monday client had a corporate culture that tolerated individuals pushing personal agendas, working in silos and disintegrated teams, commanding and controlling manners of working, and making chaos their accepted way of dealing with challenges. The Tuesday client had a corporate culture that allowed for respectful, open-minded discussion about challenges, issues, conclusions, and new directions. They were respectful, curious, honest, and vulnerable in the way they treated one another. The end results of the two approaches yielded clear, dramatic differences.

The biggest short-term difference was the speed, innovation, and efficiency at which the two different companies came to conclusions and implemented the work. As we moved forward, the Monday client had to go back to the beginning and engage in additional research involving more stakeholder teams, and they transitioned through several rounds of edits, refinements, revision, and review. This took place over a period of four months of internal discussions to decide as a team which strategic direction made most sense for the organization. They spent a great deal of time and money getting on the same page and settling on an agreed strategy. Throughout the entire process, there were constant internal challenges and power struggles, and one leader on the team quit in the process.

In comparison, the Tuesday client spent roughly one-third of the amount of time that the Monday client did coming to a conclusive strategic direction and had already begun implementing aspects of the direction, while the Monday client was struggling to get on the same page. Surprisingly or not, the Tuesday client was far more open to out-of-the-box thinking, wide ranges of innovation approaches, and atypical ways of including their culture and customers in the process and ultimately expressing their brand. They invited experimentation and creativity without trepidation and were highly collaborative in the process. They allowed for a healthy amount of chaos to take place because they had a solid culture and leadership foundation. They trusted themselves and one another. When it came down to it, they understood the essence of who they were, and they weren't afraid to express it confidently to the world.

The longer-term effects were also dramatically different. With the Monday client team, five months after the strategic work, the CEO resigned, and the VP of marketing was replaced when the new CEO took their position. The work was essentially never fully implemented because of these changes at the top of the organization. By contrast, the Tuesday client team revealed a 17 percent increase in new customers, a 21 percent increase in customer retention, and higher employee engagement, which lowered turnover by 6 percent year over year. A year later, even in the midst of the recession, their earnings report noted an increase in profit by 8.4 percent.

In both situations, I got to know several of the various leaders, including the CEOs of each company. I spent time with each of the CEOs both in group meetings and in private meetings. While it took me some time to realize it, it became clear that their leadership styles couldn't have been more different. The contrast between them boiled down to purpose, values, and vision.

The Monday client CEO and leadership team valued short-term profit above all—all conversations and considerations landed on the profit goal. This CEO saw their company as a money-generating machine and treated the team and customers as levers, cogs, and gears in that machinery. They valued the mechanisms that drove profit over people. They referred to their customers as targets and employees as resources. The Tuesday client CEO, by contrast, saw people as the life force of the business. He took time to get to know both his customers and his team members by name. I remember during a one-on-one meeting that he told me he felt it was important to reach the hearts of the team and customers, not just their mind. He was, I later learned, a student of servant leadership. He supported his team, cheered them on, challenged them when necessary, and asked for their perspective and opinions. In turn, his people lived the organizational values, were focused and loyal to him, and had an overall vision to serve their customers' needs. This contrast in clients taught me valuable lessons in leadership, culture, brand, and outcomes.

Insights, Correlations, and My Evolution

I have experienced over and over again how different cultures show up to solve challenges and confront opportunities. Years of active noticing in client relationships and experimentation on new approaches in my work with them led to my own evolution that slowly emerged somewhere in the midst of running and growing my agency business over those twenty-three years. My team and I worked with a wide variety of businesses ranging from global Fortune 100 companies to large consumer electronics and products organizations to professional sports franchises to institutions of higher education, to government agencies, to start-up businesses, small businesses, and nonprofits. Many are brands that you've heard of, while some are largely unknown outside their industry.

Through my close work serving global clients, I studied the correlations in how business leaders approached leadership and culture. I looked at the degree to which leaders and teams were self-aware and the clarity with which they understood and activated their beliefs. I noticed the similarities and differences in their guiding principles and rules of engagement in teams and the attributes of the business culture that defined how they worked with, communicated with, and treated one another. I examined how they defined success that included bottom-line health and growth, team engagement, recruitment and reviews, and employee and customer satisfaction. I looked at how they approached product development and innovation. I noticed how they approached how they created and maintained relationships with their customers.

The first link I saw was working with the global brand director of one of the world's largest entertainment companies. This leader was initially in charge of the boy's products division and was later promoted. As I worked closely with and studied this leader, he had a close, trusting relationship with everyone on the team. His bosses trusted him with wide boundaries to explore innovation and achieve results. His reports worked closely with him and were given equal amounts of explorative room to roam. The creative leaders that he worked with included the director James Cameron and John Lasseter of Pixar. Suffice to say, there was a great deal at stake in the work we were doing together.

My team and I trusted him because he seemed clear about what his values were, how they aligned with the organization's values, and how that applied to the work at hand, including but not limited to how our collective work affected the world of the brand's customers. He had the ability to be direct and transparent in feedback and goal setting. He enlisted the insight of those around him, freely and often. He encouraged his team to explore uncommon approaches. He asked thoughtful, open-ended questions that encouraged deeper consideration and widened the horizon of what was possible. He allowed for healthy amounts of chaos all in the framework that formed wide-ranging possible outcomes. He was both a big picture thinker and connector of people. He was kind, generous, curious, vulnerable, personable, passionate, daring, caring, and unassuming. He was humble yet strong. He encouraged his team beyond boundaries and let them know he had their back. He inspired when necessary and corrected when needed. He was highly creative without an ego-drive for recognition, which was a paradox for many I experienced at his level of leadership.

For me, he was the working example of a self-aware leader who served the team, the company, the partners, the audience, the community, the brand, and the purpose. In our years of working together on many projects, he became the comparative benchmark for how to thoughtfully lead for great results.

If you're anything like me, once I experience a deep truth, I can't unsee it. Once I was aware of how this leader led, I compared all other leadership approaches to his.

In my deep noticing and cataloging of how leaders worked, I realized this evolved way of leadership and doing business was a rare commodity. Time and time again, through contrasting experiences in working with different kinds of leaders, I noticed links in how they led and shaped organizations and the business outcomes that were associated with leadership beliefs and behaviors.

The stories I shared about the Monday and Tuesday Teams are based on real events, and they are anecdotal to summarize the contrast in approaches. They exemplify what I learned through close observations in working with more than two hundred fifty businesses over twenty-five-plus years. They led me not just to ideas of what a beautiful business is and can be but also to the following principles that sum them up.

The closer I looked at this way of evolved leading, the more I was drawn to focus my work in helping leaders and organizations evolve. I also realized I couldn't do this the way I wanted to run an agency. I had outevolved why the company I founded and grew existed. When I realized this, I took the steps to merge it with another company and moved on to the work I wanted to do next: helping to evolve leaders, teams, and brands into beautiful businesses.

As I analyzed and mapped the key components of evolving leadership, I saw this pattern emerge with the healthiest of companies.

Until we make the unconscious
conscious, it will direct our life
and we will call it fate.

— CARL JUNG

Eleven Junctures to a Beautiful Business

As I noted previously, the beautiful business is a spiral journey, a way of being in business, and an evolution that self-aware business leaders embark upon. Over time, I've paid close attention and taken note of key junctures that businesses experience through their evolution. These junctures are presented as signposts along the way of evolving. They are here for you to orient you and your team.

1. Self-awareness leads to evolved leaders.
2. Self-aware and evolved leaders have clarified purpose, vision, and values, which, activated consistently over time, create belonging.
3. Evolved leaders create integrated teams and beautiful cultures that are clear and aligned with their beliefs and behaviors.
4. Integrated teams work in harmony with their beliefs and serve the people connected with the organization.
5. People in groups who are connected through aligned values create and deepen belonging.
6. Belonging builds trust and love.
7. Belonging creates bonds that unify around a cause or purpose.
8. When a team is unified around a cause, it becomes ignited in their work.
9. When a united and ignited team goes about their work, they create magnetism.
10. When a united team is ignited in a cause, they become formidable.
11. The felt sense of magnetism that comes from a unified team ignited in a common cause is beauty.

Relating back to the Tuesday team, when the leadership team had aligned themselves in a set of driving beliefs, they had activated a secret weapon in creating an engaged culture. This was an organization where people knew why the organization existed and what the company was setting out to do. The organization's beliefs attracted like-minded and like-hearted views that drove harmonic behaviors. Ultimately, this led to creating innovations in products and services that ignited value to customers. And the congruent beliefs led to treating customers with a sense of service to their wants, needs, aspirations, dreams, and desires. A valuable business helps their customers realize a potential they couldn't without the products or services of that company.

What I noticed over years and decades was the more a culture was aligned in its intentional service to a customer base, the more that culture and the business thrived. It showed up in the company's ability to attract and retain loyal customers. This is a model in which service creates value.

Conversely, when companies and leaders had an unclear purpose or true north, this led to a dysfunctional culture of people and teams with segregated and sometimes competitive agendas. Or worse, if a company was clear that its primary driving motivation was to maximize profit alone, then it created a win-at-all costs culture that encouraged fear-based behavior. In turn, chaos, fear, and competition stifled innovation because employees were motivated by short-term profit generation alone. We call this greed. Its siblings are wrath, envy, pride, gluttony, and lust. While there may be attempts to conceal these attributes, they will affect how people see your company and brand.

While I admit that I was hired by some of these companies for marketing purposes, if the company lacked the awareness of where their beliefs stood, their customers eventually discovered the gaps between their stated beliefs and their actions, regardless of how good my marketing was. The character of an organization is motivated by leadership beliefs.

These brands were the ones who would chase after customers with discounts, incentives, and promotions. Some would deploy marketing funnels lined with fear, which is an emotion used to spread online ideas. Pageview marketing—tactics applied to social media and journalistic marketing—manipulates people with primal human forces. The approach takes the audience at their worst, plays on their emotions, and stokes their fire further. This is marketing that is centered on fear-based tactics designed to disrupt, alarm, and enrage customers with the purpose of capturing viewer's lizard-brain attention and motivating them to share their outrage.

Sound familiar? As consumers, it should, because this is the way so many organizations market to all of us today.

My awakening emerged when I realized this correlation. Because I don't like manipulating people into forced decisions, I stopped doing it.

The more I understood this relationship between manipulation and action, the more I wanted to serve businesses and their leaders who were committed to activating their own aligned beliefs to serve the people—employees and customers—who were connected to the organization. It was at this point that I merged the marketing side to my agency with another group and committed to my own path of shepherding awakening leaders as an advisor and consultant.

Aware and Evolving—Lessons on Insight

As I tell these contrasting stories of the Monday and Tuesday Teams, it's probably obvious that the contrast in leadership styles and, therefore, corporate cultures made all the difference in both the process and the outcomes. Slowly, I realized that the Tuesday client had hired and nurtured a team of leaders who had what Dr. Tasha Eurich, author of *Insight*, calls self-awareness.

As I've studied these contrasting experiences and hundreds of other teams and cultures over the years, it's become clear to me that the biggest differences in defining good or great leadership and teams boils down to self-awareness. As I've said previously, better people make better leaders. Expanding on this notion, more self-aware people make more self-aware cultures, which makes better teams. Consistent self-awareness applied over time to the business culture evolves into belonging, harmony, and magnetism.

Dr. Eurich and her team define self-awareness as the ability to understand who we are, how others see us, and how we fit into the world. And in her insightful book, she highlights that there are two types of self-awareness.

The first type is referred to as *internal self-awareness*. This indicates how clearly we know our own values, passions, and aspirations, how we fit with our environment, and what our impact is on others and their reactions. This includes awareness of our passion, purpose, values, motivations, thoughts, feelings, behaviors, strengths, and weaknesses.

The second type is *external self-awareness*, which is defined by an understanding of how other people view us in terms of factors listed above—including values, passions, aspirations, etc. This external self-awareness includes our awareness of how our behaviors affect the people around us. People with high external self-awareness have a clearer understanding of how their behaviors are seen and perceived by the people in their lives.

The two parts of self-awareness are independent of each other. A person can be high on external self-awareness and low on internal, or vice versa. Or they can be low or high on both types.

What's There for the Self-Aware

Dr. Eurich's research shows the following correlations:

- That people who know how others see them are more skilled at showing empathy and taking others' perspectives.
- Leaders who see themselves through the reality of their employees tend to have a better employee relationship, feel more satisfied with them as leaders, and see them as generally more effective.
- Self-awareness is the foundation for high performance, intelligent choices, and lasting relationships for leaders and employees.

However, self-reporting isn't always effective. Dr. Eurich's research shows that most people don't see themselves very clearly. "Our data reveals that 95 percent of people believe they are self-aware, but the real number is 12 to 15 percent," she says. "That means, on a good day, about 80 percent of people are lying about themselves—to themselves."[14]

Signposts to Self-Aware People

- They know the values and principles they want to live their lives by, and they work to consistently apply these values to how they live.
- They know their passions—the things that drive their motivations and get them fired up about life and work.
- They know their aspirations, including what they want to accomplish in life and the kinds of experiences they want out of life.
- They understand where they belong. They are clear about what type of environment is going to make them thrive and feel fulfilled.
- They know their patterns and their consistent ways of behavior. This essentially means they have an understanding of their character and personality.
- By embracing the previous signposts, they have a clear understanding of their impact on the people around them.

The good news is that self-awareness can be developed and improved with willingness. The first steps are self-reflection, asking for feedback, and accepting the reality of what you hear, see, and learn.

Some years ago, I hired an executive coach to help me evolve as a leader. I've hired several over the years, but this particular coach employed a 360-degree assessment, including interviewing key team members and a few of my key clients. What I wanted to understand, as much as I could, is where my blind spots existed. One of the findings that came back to me was a relatively hard pill to swallow. While I thought I was being thoughtful and conscientious as a leader, I learned that not everyone on my team saw it that way. The feedback was that I was too "hands-on with some team members" and "too hands-off with others." It seems I had some control issues with team members. I overcontrolled people in positions that were client-facing, wanting to ensure, or over insure, the account team was taking care of the client. The team members I was too hands-off with were the ones that sat outside of my expertise, including development and tech team members. I gave them too little attention and too little direction. This created the sense that I played favorites, which was not my intention. By looking at my blind spots, I became clearer about how my actions affected those around me.

Questioning my assumptions about myself and asking for feedback are part of the ongoing path of self-awareness. It takes courage to be vulnerable. Like most people, I don't find it particularly easy to hear critical feedback. I can train myself to become open to it by seeing it as a path for improvement, the road of my own evolution. But I've learned that some of the best feedback I'll ever receive is honest critique from people who know me well and have my best interests at heart. I find that pushing past the discomfort and stepping into the zone of fierce vulnerability and radical acceptance is a road to facing reality. The alternative is the road of delusion. One doorway to self-awareness is the desire to discover the truth. After all, I can't fix or improve what I'm not aware of. The solution to any problem begins with knowing you have one. Most of the best things in life, including personal growth, lie just on the other side of our discomfort. This is especially true for the road to self-awareness.

Building on Self-Awareness

As I share the insightful perspectives of how Dr. Eurich defines self-awareness, I want to point out the difference between a self-aware leader and an evolved one.

Leaders who have self-awareness are ones who have the ability to understand who we are, how others see us, and how we affect the people around us. Evolving leaders build on self-awareness with a knowing of how to apply it in their work, life, and business. Leaders have a unique view and set of responsibilities in that others look to us to set direction, orient to a vision, and define a path for realizing that vision. Having self-awareness is the entry card to great leadership, but growing your business into a beautiful one requires an individual evolution. Evolution builds on self-awareness and applies it to organizational awareness with the key driver of a clearly defined vision. Your business will never be more evolved than your own individual evolution. Conversely, your business will never outevolve the leadership of the team. Unevolved leaders hold the business back from realizing its potential. Evolving leaders keep the flow of forward growth and allow the business to keep flourishing.

Awakening leaders apply their unique stance in the world and their ability to see how they fit into the world to a knowing of how, when, and where to apply it. Awakening leaders operate from the seemingly paradoxical stances of knowing where they stand in the world and having the awakened sense of a higher calling in their work and business. Awakened leaders know their *what* and their *why*. They are aware of who they are and awake to how and why they want to apply it.

Create the highest, grandest vision possible for your life because you become what you believe.

— OPRAH WINFREY

CHAPTER 6

Leaders Choose Their Game of Business

The Unique Perch of the Leader (Evolved Leadership)

My life as a business leader exists on a unique plateau. I look out upon a vast horizon that has a vista yet to be fully shaped. It's called the world of possibility. All business leaders stand at this same unique plateau.

It's a unique stance that the people with me and behind me—my colleagues, staff, partners, customers, investors—are entrusting me to create, almost out of thin air. But I know it's not vapor. It's made of the same ground I'm currently standing on, which is solid as a rock because I created that, too.

From this unique plateau, we all have a choice in how we see and engage with our world. Ultimately, there are two ways I can play the game of business.

The competitive game of short-term wins is played by the people on Wall Street who are focused on making a profit next Wednesday. This is the *win-at-all-cost* game that takes a scarcity mentality to play, where the world is seen as a competitive landscape and those that play this game will do anything it takes to win.

Indicators of those that play the *competitive game* (a.k.a. the *short game*, the *scarcity game*, the *commodity game*):

- Anyone not with you is against you.
- The competition is the enemy.
- Customers are dollar signs to be won through promotions, discounts, and incentives.
- You settle for "yes" people and good soldiers who fall in line.
- Customers are expected to evaporate at the next wind of change.

We've all read the headlines of companies and people who've played this game. Banks who drive their employees to unnecessarily oversell products to customers just to increase their earnings statement. Start-ups that promise integrity to customers but have unfair or abusive cultures. Auto companies who cheat on emissions reporting just to report better gas mileage. Fast-growing companies that falsely claim earnings just to boost stock valuation. But make no mistake: playing this type of game in business is a choice. They don't have to play this way and neither do you.

In 1987, James P. Carse wrote *Finite and Infinite Games*, on which Simon Sinek based his 2020 book *The Infinite Game*. "In the finite games," Sinek argues, "like football or chess, the players are known, the rules are fixed, and the endpoint is clear. The winners and losers are easily identified."[15]

Sinek continues: "In infinite games, like business or politics or life itself, the players come and go, the rules are changeable, and there is no defined endpoint. There are no winners or losers in an infinite game; there is only ahead and behind."[16]

A beautiful business plays the infinite game, which can also be referred to as the abundance game, the cooperative game, and the long game.

This version of the game is played by people who are in it for the long haul—people who want to create value for customers, investors, and staff. It's played by people with an abundance and growth mindset; those who see the world as a place where there are endless resources available. When we play the game of the beautiful business, we collaborate with as many good people as we can to do great work for and with the world.

Warren Buffett invests in these types of companies. Blake Mycoskie has created them. So have Yvon Chouinard, Sarah Blakely, Oprah Winfrey, Rebekah Neumann, Tony Hsieh, and Ben Cohen and Jerry Greenfield.

The long game is a *value-centric game* where value is constantly generated and then improved upon for your customers, investors, vendors, and team. Under this model, your organizational core values are the operating system for your culture and customer service, while they also provide the core magnetism and gravitational pull that attracts the kind of work your business was most intended to do.

Starting this value-centric game and building a beautiful business first requires articulating what you believe in and what you value. I write and speak a good deal about leaders and businesses getting crystal clear in what they believe because that clarity creates the trustable ground on which a business can firmly stand. Your values created your past and will create your future. Your business's values created its past and will manifest its future. If a business believes in scarcity and short-term wins, that's what it will get. If a business believes in an abundant, collaborative world, it will exist amidst that abundance.

Beliefs are a beacon, a calling, and an invitation to those who see themselves within the story of those same or similar beliefs. From a foundation of strongly held core values, any future is imaginable.

Companies that play the *short game* innovate less and often find themselves stuck in a repetitive cycle of the same thing for years. These cycles include perpetually chasing customers, replacing the unengaged, experiencing high turnover with new staff, and replicating what the competition is doing. This is an endless game of playing "catch-up."

In contrast, companies playing the long game and operating from deeply held beliefs make room for the evolution of their purpose. How that purpose takes shape might very well change a company in ways that could never have been strategized or predicted.

Leaders who play the *long game* create a long and fruitful future. Leaders who live and work from this vista are more likely to know exactly where they'll be a year from now and ten years from now and where their company will be one hundred years from now. It's very difficult to create a company that is going to be valuable a year, a decade, or a century from now by playing the *short game*.

Fusing Art and Science in Business

Leadership and entrepreneurship are as much art as science. While data can be valuable, orienting, and informative, much of what the leader works with is human dynamics—theirs and others. A good leader must be aware enough to see beyond the data and know what to do with all the information that's coming our way. We must see the truth, the reality, the humanity, the possibilities. At times, the leader follows their gut, or heart, regardless of what the data say. Ultimately, the leader must follow their own heart and ignite the activation of their soul.

Leaders with a passionate purpose tend to make most number crunchers uneasy. Most numbers-focused people are unsure how to make quantified sense of intangibles. Entrepreneurship and business leadership can be like playing live jazz. I only know enough about jazz to appreciate the long-practiced mastery and artistry that's required to play good jazz. To some, this form of music seems chaotic and formless. To others, it can feel like a daunting, multiheaded beast that most would prefer to avoid. True for both entrepreneurship and jazz musicianship, the integration of harmonic form and individualized experimentation sit at the heart of this brilliant, challenging, and highly human performance vocation.

Like entrepreneurship, great jazz requires a mind-bogglingly deep and wide skill set that includes the mastery of your instrument and the artistry to play it in a group setting and as a solo expression. It is both individualized and collaborative. It is dynamic and agile. It requires the equally important abilities to hold to the form and structure of the song that's being played, while you find your own voice as a creative and innovative improviser. Here, the musical and entrepreneurial artists experiment with keeping and breaking the structure.

This experimentation can include dissonant, collaborative, harmonic, and innovative realms while always coming back to the structured arrangement. It requires the collaborative ability to play with both harmony and disharmony with your fellow performers. Here, you play off of and cooperate with one another. It requires the ability to play with expansive technique to an attentive audience who is paying to see you perform. The jazz musician and business leader are both individual standouts and collaborative team performers.

All of this is delivered during live performance, where real jazz and entrepreneurship happens. If someone makes a mistake, the performers move on as there's more music to play, because that's what the audience has paid to experience. For those who can appreciate both the nuanced individual parts and the collective effects, when performed at its highest level, it can be a transformative experience.

Of course, everything that's required of you in business and jazz musicianship is done so only after years of intentional practice. It requires the players to be aware of their skills and the skills of those around them. It demands acute awareness of what the structure and instrument can and can't do. It necessitates the openness to explore new possibilities, the guidance of teachers, leaders, and other players, and the self-reflection to understand where your talents and abilities lie. It requires a team of trusted and trusting collaborators that allow the opportunity to take it to the stage. It also demands an enthusiastic attitude to get you through the long hours of practice, struggle, mistakes, and ever-increasing challenges. You have to want it and want to be good at it.

Mastery and its matured sibling, artistry, requires us to do all of what we do wholeheartedly. We have the intrinsic drive to do what we do at the highest levels while allowing ourselves to be transformed by the beautiful effect of the expression.

Like jazz, modern capitalism has uniquely American roots. However, you need not be American to activate, perform, embrace, or appreciate either. Both entrepreneurship and jazz can be a demanding, daunting, and ever-challenging journey that will test your resolve and reward you with transformative experiences. Performing at the highest levels means *bringing it* to the audience— moving them, transporting them, and delivering tangible and intangible value for the audience.

Human Artistry at Work

In his book *Mastery*, author Robert Greene speaks to a core truth: "Your emotional commitment to what you are doing will be translated directly into your work. If you go at your work with half a heart, it will show the lackluster results and in the laggard way you reach the end."[17] If you really want to live a beautiful life and build a beautiful business, you have to lead the kind of life that stirs your heart and soul awake. Certain activities of the business leader quiet the heart and soul, including being too analytical, too economical, too conventional, too professional, and too data-driven. While aspects of this are, of course, necessary for a healthy business, overcompensating in these areas will repress the conviction of heart and soul.

Let me dispel the notion of a safe life. This is no such thing as a fully safe investment of your time, energy, and money. You cannot control much of what life has to offer. Loving, in any form, requires vulnerability. There's no such life that journeys without some heartbreak. We are made to love what we love, be what we will be. And the richness of life can't be found within the fleeting financial measuring sticks but can be found within the fruits of love.

As Victor Frankl reminds us in *Man's Search for Meaning*, "Forces beyond your control can take away everything you possess except one thing: your freedom to choose how you will respond to the situation."[18]

To live is to love. A life or work without love at the core is a hollow venture with no promise for true fulfillment. The strategic attempt to lock away all that you want to protect in a dark, airless, motionless safe is to infuse stagnation. The only change that takes place in this lifeless chamber is to wither. In that coffin-like safe, what attempts to grow and flourish cannot. So goes the life, work, and business that attempts to lock off all it wants to protect from the harms of the world. Yes, it will try to be impenetrable, but it will also be without vitality. Entombing your heart to protect it from breaking shuts off your vitality for living the precious life you were given.

It is Mary Olivier who asks us in her famous poem "The Summer Day," "Doesn't everything die at last, and too soon? / Tell me, what is it you plan to do / with your one wild and precious life?"[19]

Leadership Artistry Pillars

The artistry of leadership calls on a leader to be a master in three key areas: mastery of awareness, mastery of visionary transformation, and mastery of purpose and love. Napoleon said that "the role of the leader is to define reality and give hope." In leadership, defining reality can be considered subjective. Steve Jobs, for instance, was famous for bending reality or living in a reality he was working to create.

My friend and colleague MaeLin Levine offers a beautiful living example of a living leadership artistry. She is the coprincipal of Visual Asylum, a design firm in San Diego, but she has also created the visionary Urban Discovery Academy (UDA). The concept for UDA emerged at the intersection of two vanguard ideas—first, to align with regional planners to invigorate the East Village section of downtown San Diego; and second, to align with progressive national education STEAM (science, technology, engineering, art, and math) paradigm. MaeLin and her founding team went well beyond the conventional model of a graphic design firm. By activating her love for design and its impact, her self-awareness as a leader, and her visionary focus to transform a neighborhood, MaeLin enhanced the lives of the families who are engaged with UDA. By envisioning a new school and building it from the ground up, even amidst the recession of 2008, MaeLin tapped into her and her team's passion and purpose-driven momentum to create an extraordinary school. Overcoming tremendous headwinds, the doors for UDA opened in 2015.

If a leader is to tap the true potential of their own work in life and their business, they must cultivate their own living artistry—a work of art as a human being, striving to create what they can create. The artist within you calls you forward to create the life you're able to live, to give more than you take, to celebrate the values within you.

The Three Pillars to Leadership Artistry

Self-Awareness. As I outlined above, self-awareness is when I am both aware of what my drivers and motivations are and aware of how the actions of my drivers affect others around me. When I confront my reality, I will begin to master the skill of self-awareness. This requires deep attentiveness on my part, and the ability to discern reality from perception, true from false.

Think of self-awareness this way. You are the driver of your vehicle.

Your internal self-awareness is your eyes on the road, hands on the steering wheel, and feet on the gas and brake pedals. This determines how you drive your car, at what speed, in which direction, and how you assess and navigate the road around you. This internal self-awareness is knowing what state you, the driver, is in. Here, you know if you're driving with road rage or with relaxed but alert diligence. You know whether or not you're alert enough to operate the vehicle and to what extent you have the skills and information required to do so safely. You know which direction and destination you're headed toward and why you're going there. You know enough about yourself, including your internal drivers and motivations, to get you and whatever passengers you might have with you to your aimed destination for an adventurous road trip that's worth the journey.

External self-awareness is knowing how your vehicle is interacting with the seen and unseen elements around you, and especially other drivers, weather conditions, and possible road obstacles. It's not enough to know how to drive your car and in which direction you drive. The driver has to know how they are interacting with the traffic and environment around them in order to travel safely, efficiently, and respectfully.

Visionary Transformation. When I see clearly the reality that's in front of me and my team, I can then cast a vision that creates a lucid future that I will transform my company toward. As that vision becomes crystalized, I can clear the way for the organization to realize this vision. I'll talk more about *vision* in chapter 7.

Purpose and Love. A higher purpose, one with integrity, is essential for having love infused within your business. When I infuse a higher purpose into my business, love is infused. When I master my company's purpose, I can therefore build a business based on love. I'll go more into purpose in the next two chapters, and I'll go deeper into what I mean by "love" in the business later in this chapter.

Mastering these three key areas forges deep bonds of belonging between a team and the purpose that team is collectively pulling together to achieve. It forms a harmonic integrity between beliefs and behaviors, inside and outside an organization, which builds trust. It creates magnetism between all the people who are aligned with the values, vision, and purpose.

> **❝ Life comes from physical survival; but the good life comes from what we care about.**
>
> — ROLLO MAY, *LOVE & WILL* (1969)

Every expedition involves making two thoughtful decisions: where to go and how to get there. Success and goal achievement are no accident. Defining how you reach your focused goals can orient the unique positioning of your business and lay the groundwork to your organization's operating system of how you do your work.

Where to go is defined by your purpose (your why) and your vision (what the world will look like as you go about achieving your purpose). How you get there is defined by your values in action, which is your organization's operating system.

Growing, nurturing, and evolving your business is about forging your own courageous and bold path, and paradoxically it is about allowing space for the possible to come into fruition and become manifest. If you have too tight a purpose and vision, your business might not be allowing for the wide range of possibilities for the magnitude of your business's potential. The leader becomes artist-like, so long as she has clear intent through a higher purpose and she infuses a healthy dose of allowing. Leaders, like artists, both create and allow.

Your business trajectory is both a journey of forging your vision and a surrendering to unseen possibilities. If we force too much, try too hard to create the only outcome we can imagine, we end up limiting the wide range of possibilities that lie ahead. Here, the artist leader can lean into the masterful improv tool of "yes, and . . ." This magical process of "yes, and . . ." builds on the current reality and allows for new creative possibilities while still holding our true north course to our envisioned purpose.

As a leader working with artistry, your way of living is shaped by your beliefs, which define your priorities and actions, which create your unique results. A beautiful business is both a creative act of claiming your birthright as a human creator and leader, and an act of defiance from the myopic and arbitrary rules that profit-only businesses operate from.

Any business will, at times, find itself challenged or struggling. With a beautiful business, we will find meaning when we will inevitably struggle. Our purpose will move us beyond that struggle, and we will be driven by an inner force. This inner force is required to create extraordinary value and make a difference in the lives of all of our stakeholders.

The healthiest businesses aren't aiming to be bigger as much as they are evolving to become more viable, valuable, and vital. It is my belief that leadership and entrepreneurship is ultimately about serving. When I approach my work, my business, and my life from a perspective of service, I aim for impact that goes beyond my own self-serving needs and wants into impact that improves the lives of all those associated with the business. This includes my employees, customers, collaborators, investors, partners, and community. When I am in service to some larger impact, I work through an intrinsic motivation set that drives me and my team to do extraordinary things.

Pulling the Rope in the Same Direction

Few things have inhibited the success of a business more than a leader stating a singular goal while not aligning their team to all pull in that direction. I see this time and time again in cultures, where there is a stated goal, vision, mission, or purpose for the organization, but the actions and behaviors within that culture are not aligned in a common direction. Chaos, confusion, and contradiction can all be inhibitors to achieving your purpose.

Conversely, there's nothing more formidable than a united group of souls ignited in a common cause, with love at the core. We've seen this through the ages: the Allies united to overcome the forces of evil in World War II; Gandhi's nonviolent leadership of India's independence movement against British rule; the NASA team bonding against great odds to put a man on the moon in the 1960s; the civil rights movement in the US led by Dr. Martin Luther King and others, who worked to overcome the injustices of racism.

When we bond together in a common cause, we can create exponential results. Our world needs this now as much as ever. The issues that we face in our world today are more global, more complex, and more daunting than ever before. Businesses that have achieved what Abraham Maslow referred to as *self-actualization* and *transcendence* can nourish the changes that the world is hungry for. This book is a calling card, an invitation, an actionable manifesto to create more beauty in everything your business comes into contact with.

Bringing Love into the Business

There's a saying that goes "You can't hate someone whose story you know." Conversely, it's hard to be hated when someone knows your story. This works on the individual level, the organizational level, and the societal level. Building bonds of belonging requires knowing and sharing the stories. The act and gift of presence, which includes the skills of empathy and deep listening, is the threshold for our ability to love them. Empathy is the ability to connect to emotions that underpin someone's experience. And deep listening is the ability to whole-body witness and be present for what people are saying and feeling.

In much of organizational life, there is an inhibition and even a denial to the power of honest and vulnerable communication. We fear that it will lead us to the path of the blame game, filled with guilt and accusations, which dismantles trust and fractures relationships. We avoid truth-telling meetings, not just because we're busy and more meetings adds to our stretched-thin time, but because what we've done for years is accuse, blame, and talk *at* one another, pushing our own agenda.

The shame and vulnerability work of Brené Brown comes to the forefront again where she notes that "empathy is a choice and it is a vulnerable choice because in order to connect with you, I have to connect with something in myself that knows that feeling."[20] It's vital to put our personal agendas aside in order to see the power of seeing and hearing the truth of other people's stories, which evolves our capacities to belong.

While there some debate about the number of forms of love the Greeks have, here I'll share the most commonly defined: **Eros**, meaning the passionate, intimate love; **Xenia**, meaning love of hospitality and guest friendship; **Storge**, meaning the affection that exists primarily between parents and children; **Philautia**, meaning the basic human necessity for self-love and regard for one's own happiness; **Agape**, meaning charity and the love of god for man and man for god; and **Philia**, meaning affection and loyalty of equals, peers, and the appreciation for the beauty within a person.[21]

When we think of love in Western culture, we often think of the eros form of love, but in the business world the expression and experience of love can show up in the forms of agape, philia, xenia, and sometimes philautia. We can experience agape when we're working from a driving purpose in our business. We can experience philia when we have a strong sense of belonging in our cultures and teams and with our customers. We can experience xenia in brands in the hospitality and human services industries. And individually we can experience philautia when we discover the depth of our self-love, fulfillment, and self-worth by aligning our vocation with our deeply held living beliefs.

As the leader of your life and your business, you are the artist, architect, author, and performer of your work. When you act with love at your core, in the appropriate forms, you can achieve more fulfilling levels of life-enhancing experiences. Each of you, whether you embrace it or not, are directly involved in the invention of your world and your work. As a highly performing business leader, you have chosen or been charged with the honorable responsibility to envision a possibility and journey yourself and your team forward into your yet-to-be-forged future. Your team is entrusting you with coherent and responsible guidance. In the adventure toward this future, you are aligning the necessary, diverse, and unarranged elements required to reach this envisioned destination into an integrated whole.

> **❝ I'm always thinking about creating. My future starts when I wake up in the morning and see the light.**
>
> — MILES DAVIS

The Beautiful Culture, Igniting in a Common Cause

When we bond together in a common cause, we create exponential results. Our world needs this now as much as ever. The issues that we face in our world today are more global, more complex, and more daunting than ever before.

When leaders tap into their own evolution, the next logical and actionable step is to involve the team around them, regardless of size, into a unified force. Again, I think of how nature can be a vital model for how to create a unified culture.

There's a long-standing law in Ireland called the Bretha Comaithchesa or "Laws of the Neighborhood."[22] These laws served the Irish people up to the seventeenth century and predate the Magna Carta. In these laws of neighborhood, the resources of the forest belonged to every person on the condition that they took only what they needed. No more, no less. This law spoke with the attitude of abundance of natural resources and the symbiotic nature of all natural elements. Within this system, community members worked in unison to ensure that all their neighbors were cared for and the resources they drew upon were equally cared for. This requires an agreement from the community to honor each other, nature, and the cooperative connection of all orchestrated elements.

This law system came from the observation that nature is a near-perfect model for society and culture. Nature, the forests, and gardens arrange themselves from the very biggest to the smallest creatures, which all play their own vital role in the symbiotic whole. And all ingredients are all are working together in harmony.

In the best of organizational cultures I've seen operate with great efficiency, the whole is as important as the largest and smallest parts. Some of the smaller parts of our cultures are considered the soft skills that define how humans interact with one another. As most leaders now understand, it's the soft skills where the real work gets done or doesn't. In the Monday client story shared previously, the leaders led through a command-and-control system. They bypassed their attention from necessary soft skills to ensure the team was aligned, had trust, fostered strong communication, and held each other accountable for their behaviors and outcomes and the manner in which they collaborated. This yielded unwelcome results. Conversely, I've noticed this pattern time and time again: when company leaders nurture the symbiotic nature of the largest and smallest parts of the team, the culture flourishes. Just like a gardener who cares for the soil, seeds, weeds, plants, bugs, nutrients, and watering, these gardens flourish—creating greater yields and greater beauty.

Humanity and the Beautiful Business

Entrepreneurship and all forms of artistry are deeply human expressions— beautiful in the way they exemplify the dualistic nature that defines our humanity. As humans, we are one part animal and, as such, inextricably connected to the systems and rhythms of our natural world. This animalistic side of us has the hunter-gatherer drive to work with the natural elements and resources around us to make a living and create our world.

The other part of our humanity is animated by unseen and mystical forces that underscore our awareness of and curiosity for the mysteries of being human. The nature of humanity is a creative nature. We're all born creatives. And if we're attuned to it, we can live in the world of possibilities.

We humans are inseparably tethered both to each other and, at the same time, our natural world. We leaders of a beautiful business bring all of our humanity forward into performance and expression. We create our world in synergistic collaboration with those who share our worldview. In doing so, we perform wholeheartedly in concert with our aligned deeply held beliefs.

Here's the paradox: your expressed humanity—and business—is unique to you and inextricably connected to all other humans, all living things, and to the unseen animating origins that drive your cravings, convictions, and connections. There's nothing more powerful than a united group of souls ignited in a common cause with love at its core.

Putting It All Together

> **❝ To be Great, Be Entire**
>
> **To be great, be entire:**
>
> **Of what is your nothing**
>
> **Exaggerated or exclude**
>
> **Be whole in each thing. Put all that you are**
>
> **Into the least that you do**
>
> **Like that on each place the whole moon**
>
> **Shines for she lives aloft.**
>
> — FERNANDO PESSOA

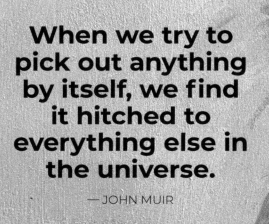

When we try to pick out anything by itself, we find it hitched to everything else in the universe.

—JOHN MUIR

The late Buckminster Fuller noted that "synergy is to energy as integration is to differentiation."[23] What he was speaking about was his way of seeing and appreciating life. Fuller continues: "In order to be able to understand the great complexity of life and to understand what the universe is doing, the first word to learn is synergy." Synergy defines how the whole system operates in congruence with the behavior of their parts. "It is synergy," he notes, "that holds our earth together with the moon; and it is synergy which holds our universe together."[24]

In work and in life, everything we do has a cumulative effect. Even the word *corporation* bears its roots from the Latin word *corporare*, meaning to "combine in one body" or "persons united in a body for some common purpose." There is little we do in the business world that is completely alone. Even if you're a solopreneur, you still have a customer to serve and an audience to commune with. A corporation is defined by something that one cannot do alone and must therefore work within an integrated system that involves both collaborations and unified outcomes. The outcomes that we create in our life and work are done so by the summation of our actions, driven by our individual and collective beliefs, and applied consistently over time.

What you believe, whether you're conscious of it or not, is orchestrated in an expressed synergistic and connected pattern. The more you become aware of and intentionally act within your own operating system of working and living, the more exponential your results. In this case, synergistic consciousness acts as a straightened line rather than an indirect, meandering approach to your intended outcomes.

> **❝ I think one of the most misunderstood things about business in America is that people are either doing things for altruistic reasons or they are greedy and selfish, just after profit. That type of dichotomy portrays a false image of business . . . The whole idea is to do both.**
>
> —JOHN MACKEY

My Awakening Journey Continued

When I founded my agency in 1994, I had very little clue what I was doing or why I was doing it. Thus, I set out on a course to go beyond skilled designer and strategist and learn how to be in business. As I grew my business, I needed to grow, too. The realization came quickly that I knew very little about the mechanics of running a business, building predictable systems and structures so I could manage an entity that had some foundation. I read countless books on business, business development, leadership, and management, and I hired consultants and coaches to accelerate my learning.

My awakening, like any earned wisdom, didn't happen in a flash. The movie version of the moment of truth can happen, but that's not how it occurred for me. Regardless of the time it took, when I awakened, my entire worldview changed. There was no going back once certain fundamental truths revealed themselves. Unseeing them was impossible.

There were a few key junctures, influences, and people that resonated with me on my path. These include David C. Baker, whose constant drumbeating about expertise and the activated value of writing to explore what you think and believe encouraged me to get clear about what I was doing and why. There were many guides, mentors, coaches, counselors, and consultants that I worked with over time. There were also countless books that I read on leadership, business, management, and personal transformation. While there are far too many names and books to list here, a few stand out as perennial influencers: Brené Brown, Elizabeth Gilbert, Maya Angelou, Dan Pink, Jim Collins, John O'Donohue, Ryan Holiday, Toni Morrison, Pema Chodron, James Baldwin, David Brooks, Parker Palmer, Langston Hughes, Mary Oliver, W. E. B. Du Bois, Wendell Berry, Thomas Merton, Daniel Siegel, Robert Greene, Gay Hendricks, Seth Godin, and Steven Pressfield. There was also the hands-on work I did with the poet-philosopher David Whyte, his faculty, and my cohort, whom I worked with for a year in Whidbey Island to explore the depths of conversational leadership, the poetic sensitivities of nuanced language, and application of living artistry. Also important were my continued studies of Joseph Campbell, Abraham Maslow, Carl Jung, and Marcus Aurelius.

My journey includes many years of hard looks in the mirror, daily meditation and contemplation, and a deep and ongoing study of myself and those that influenced me. It also includes the learning and influence of working alongside thousands of business leaders that allowed me to collect enough experiential data to come to this realization: people who do the hard work of their own personal evolution make better leaders. To be evolved is to be conscious of who you are and your impact on the world around you. It is to be aware that you have to do your own work in order to lead others to their own potential.

❝ Enlightened leadership is spiritual if we understand spirituality not as some kind of religious dogma or ideology but as the domain of awareness where we experience values like truth, goodness, beauty, love and compassion, and also intuition, creativity, insight and focused attention.

— DEEPAK CHOPRA

The Journey to Evolved Leadership

It's lonely at the top, so the saying goes. Entrepreneurs and business leaders face a unique set of challenges. Having led companies for twenty-five years and counting, and working with many business leaders, I know the stress and pressure that work creates is significant and near constant. I also know that leadership starts with the self. The more I do the work of knowing and improving myself, the better I am as a leader. However, it's only lonely at the top if I isolate myself from the people around me and my surroundings.

One of the unstated laws at work is to check your whole self at the door. In many business cultures, we're not supposed to bring our humanity to work. A 2013 Deloitte study found that 61 percent of employees "cover" their identities in some way and downplay parts of themselves.[25] The term "covering," coined in 1963 by sociologist Erving Goffman, describes how individuals with stigmatized identities or identity attributes go to great effort to keep that stigma from looming large. This might include someone's identity as a parent or their sexual preference. People "cover" due to the fear that they'll be discriminated against in the workplace.

Leaders are expected to have all the answers, to keep it all together, to be—or be seen as—perfect. But you know that's impossible. We bring all of ourselves to work, even if we don't express it or share it all. The things that shaped our upbringing, the realms where our beliefs are formed, and the level to which we all do the work on adulting ourselves all show up in the leadership realm. Becoming a good leader is directly connected to becoming a good adult. Our personal growth is inextricable to our leadership potential. A dysfunctional person can't be a great leader.

When we enhance our understanding of who we are, what we think we know, and what our driving beliefs are, we consciously apply them to all that we do. When you are living and working in a high state of an integrated life, you are able to face the bottomless uncertainty that paints your vocational landscape. When you enhance your life with a resounding *why*, you are able to face the many uncertainties in the array of *hows*.

Leading organizations and teams can become a place for us to learn about our blind spots, shortcomings, talents, and gifts. The work of our personal evolution can illuminate our potential as whole humans at work and elsewhere. There is a shortage of leadership books that focus on evolving the whole person. While it can feel lonely at the top, it's important to remember you're not alone. All leaders are in the same boat as you—going about your work at work and going about your life as you live it. Growth happens with intention, insight, hard work, and introspection.

As previously shared, my evolution began when I slowly realized there was a stark difference between businesses that are led by evolved individuals and those that are still evolving. Companies led by these types of evolved individuals were the ones that had healthier cultures, more engaged teams, and stronger bonds with their customers. Just as leaders should be aligning the smallest and largest parts of their business, they need to make room for individuals to grow and evolve. As I stated before, no organization, including its culture, will outevolve the leader or leaders on the team. That team's ability to bring the bulk of the team into an ever-evolving state will have a direct effect on the collective success of the organization.

And the more I understood the correlation that more evolved people make better leaders, the more I wanted to apply this to my own world and vocation. This correlative insight amplified my desire to evolve personally. As I evolved, my leadership stance evolved. I then committed myself to serving evolving leaders as an advisor and consultant with the singular focus to help people create, build, and grow evolved brands and cultures and ultimately beautiful businesses.

> **❝ To have a firm persuasion in our work—to feel that what we do is right for ourselves and good for the world at the exact same time—is one of the great triumphs of human existence.**
>
> — DAVID WHYTE

Beauty and Leadership

Part of the beauty of leadership is that we all get to decide for ourselves what our beliefs, practices, and standards are. What works for Yvon Chouinard is different from what works for Oprah Winfrey, which is different from what works for Richard Branson. What leaders must do is strive for their own personal improvement and align that with the clarity of knowing who they are now and what matters most to them. Good leaders must love themselves (the *philautia* form of love). I have noticed a few common keys to good or great leadership. These include self-awareness, empathy, presence, vision, purpose, integrity, humility, and compassion. These evolved leadership qualities, among others that you may count as significant or nonnegotiable, tend to create organizations and teams that have the core tenets of a beautiful business: belonging, integrity, and magnetism.

What's at stake with leadership is decidedly high. Your people look to you to lead them through the brightest and darkest of days, and set the vision and priorities, which have direct and exponential effects on their lives and the lives of their family. How you lead them can lead to either great or unintendedly bad outcomes. The risks you take are not just your risks but the risks of the well-being of the organization and the livelihoods that are at stake. The stakes turn even higher when the evolved leader throws down the gauntlet of going beyond profit alone to create outcomes of greater significance. In order to create something that matters, something of significant value, something that stands the test of time, leaders must be driven by an equally powerful inner force and outer focus. The rewards of sacrifice that come from a higher purpose expand to exponential outcomes.

Leading at its heart takes courage. And courage takes heart. The word *courage* emerges from the Old French word *cœur*, meaning heart. Once we ignite the clarity of doing work that's important, we tether our heartfelt work with a purpose-driven achievement set. Part of the beauty is that your purpose, in life or in work, will never be fully realized. This can be both daunting and inspiring, for there's always more work to do in realizing our potential as humans and as leaders. This best version of work is truly never-ending. As such, we can see it much more of a journey, or as David Whyte or John O'Donohue would call it, a pilgrimage.

In his book *The Obstacle Is the Way*, Ryan Holiday points out that "what matters most is not what these obstacles are but how we see them, how we react to them, and whether we keep our composure."[26] The light that summons us through the tunnel of our journey is what encourages us forward through our darkest and most challenging of times. With something more significant in our focus than simply income or profit, we respond differently. When our higher purpose is deeply infused in our business, we can fend off the seemingly insurmountable forces that surround us.

In his book *Crossing the Unknown Sea*, David Whyte tells a potent story of a moment of self-inquiry with Benedictine monk Brother David Steindl-Rast. As the story goes, David Whyte had just returned home to spend time with Brother David after a particularly difficult week of work in the nonprofit he was serving at the time. With a couple of glasses of freshly poured wine on the table, Whyte says to Brother David, "Tell me about exhaustion."

Brother David's response was surprising. "You know that the antidote to exhaustion is not necessarily rest?"

"The antidote to exhaustion is not necessarily rest," David Whyte repeated. "What is it, then?"

"The antidote to exhaustion is wholeheartedness," Brother David said. He continued. "You are so tired through and through because a good half of what you do here in this organization has nothing to do with your true powers, or the place you have reached in your life. You are only half here, and half here will kill you after a while. You need something to which you can give your full powers. You know what that is; I don't have to tell you."[27]

What Brother David didn't have to say was that he knew David Whyte wanted his work to be about his poetry.

In this story, there is a direct reference to a Rilke poem entitled "The Swan."[28]

> This clumsy living that moves lumbering
> as if in ropes through what is not done,
> reminds us of the awkward way the swan walks.
> And to die, which is the letting go
> of the ground we stand on and cling to every day,
> is like the swan, when he nervously lets himself down
> into the water, which receives him gaily
> and which flows joyfully under
> and after him, wave after wave,
> while the swan, unmoving and marvelously calm,
> is pleased to be carried, each moment more fully grown,
> more like a king, further and further on.

Discovering the Wholehearted You

We all have had moments or perhaps years where we fought against the natural forces around us, only to realize that the place where we were instilling the fight was not our place at all. We didn't belong there. We didn't belong to the work or the place or the people or the environment. We suffered from unfound wholeheartedness due to misalignment. Our own unique form of beauty in leadership is both finding or creating that place where all of our genuine skill sets that make us uniquely us come together in a confluence of grace and all of this applied in the right direction and purpose. There is a genius, a grace, and an unquestionable beauty to something that is completely and fully itself. Like the swan that finds the trustable place where it's meant to be, and from there floats and takes flight untethered by common forces, we, too, are called home to this place where we truly belong and not just fit in. Genius in this sense can be something that is completely itself.

True beauty-infused leadership involves creating something that's real from a conjured vision that's built on trustable ground. Some of the unspoken parts of leadership involve tethering the rich unseen inner world filled with deep beliefs and imagination with the yet-to-be-created outer world of possibilities informed by realities. Evolving leaders are either completely conscious of their beliefs that build trustable ground on which they stand or are creating the clarity of what that trustable ground is made of. This is what real genius and real beauty at work is: a meeting of who we're meant to be in the world and how we're meant to live and work in the world.

Perhaps we are awake to the fact that, in the end, we ourselves are a gift to the world. Perhaps we know full well that our gifts should not be squandered on meaningless work but rather invested into endeavors that make the world of our people a better place. And perhaps the greatest, most beautiful gift we can give to the world is the truest, most authentic version of ourselves aimed at the highest purpose we can imagine. Our individual potential—the very best we personally are capable of—is the highest measure of a wholehearted life. Our wholehearted human imagination, after all, is the conduit between what is and what can be.

What Keeps Leaders Up at Night

Some time ago while running an executive leadership offsite, the CEO asked me a poignant question.

"The biggest challenge we're facing in our organization is change—change in the market landscape and change in the ways we recruit, hire, and keep employees engaged. How will going through this brand evolution program help us address these changes?"

Fair question.

Here's my response.

"To address both issues, you need to make it about people and beliefs. Because a brand is ultimately about your business's character, it's a people issue. It's about your people and your customers—what you both believe and how you are connected to one another."

The CEO leaned back in his chair, silent. His eyes moved back and forth, as though reevaluating everything he had been considering up to that point.

Bingo. Here is something he had not yet considered.

And I continued. "What you care about defines how you do business. How you do business and the value that creates for your customers defines who's attracted to you. This brand program will mine and activate your beliefs. It will put the spotlight on your values and your value to customers. We're going to create your unique brand gravity."

Evolving your brand is an investment in your beautiful business. A true brand evolution takes a business to its next level of opportunity and growth. Leaders I work with are looking for clear business outcomes from a brand evolution. They want to see the connections between their brand investment, their short- and long-term health, and the profit and impact centers within their businesses. They need their problems solved.

Rightly so. It's their job and my job, too. Often business leaders look to hire me to address what appears to be short-term business challenges like positioning, marketing, changes in market landscape, or new market competitors. But the best business and life strategies I've seen and work on essentially boil down to long-term thinking and planning. As such, I work to encourage businesses to strategize, think, plan, and act as long-term as possible.

The impetus behind most business evolution usually begins with an economic goal. And it's ultimately a *people thing*—culture, customers, partners, investors, donors. It's no longer enough for brands to just deliver a decent product, look good, and be seen. Consumers and employees are insistent on being aligned with meaningful attributes that create an alignment in values. They want to be connected to the beliefs of your brand. They want to belong to it. If they don't, they'll go elsewhere and search for a brand that they do belong to.

Only when economic circumstances are painful enough—loss in market-share, diminished reputation, lost opportunities to reach a larger audience, or customers switching to a more meaningful competitor brand—do business leaders take the courageous step of a brand evolution. The good news is there are solutions.

What to do? Here are my suggestions:

- Get seriously clear about the real reason you're in business—your why, your true north, your reason for being. Then capture it, communicate it, and commit to it.
- Once you've mined and articulated your organizational beliefs (your purpose, vision, values, and promise), take a stand for them—and go public with them.
- Turn your beliefs into actionable and accountable behaviors throughout your organization. Then measure how well you live up to them.
- Know your real customer and be courageous in articulating your POV so they get you and you show that you understand them.
- Create better (more humanized) marketing that is less about selling and more about creating long-term customer relationships. Listen to what they have to say.
- Be real. Be honest. And work to earn the trust of your people (inside and outside).
- Kill a portion of your ad budget and invest that money into your people and innovation.
- Reconfigure your recruitment, vetting, hiring, and training practices to ensure you're bringing on the right people for the right roles.
- Get over the notion that your customers are easily replaced and instead focus on caring for them by providing greater, deeper, and richer value.

Some startling statistics from Edelman:[29]

- Sixty-four percent of people say that CEOs should take the lead on change rather than waiting for the government to impose it.
- One in two people are belief-driven buyers. They choose, switch, avoid, or boycott a brand based on its stand on societal issues.
- Sixty-seven percent of people bought from a brand for the first time because of its position on a controversial issue.
- Sixty percent of people agree that brands should make it easier for me to see what their values and positions on important issues are when I am about to make a purchase.
- Fifty-six percent of people agree that marketers spend too much time looking for ways to force me to pay attention to their messages and not enough time thinking of ways to make me want to pay attention.

The Questions for Leaders: What Kind of Leader Are You?

What kind of leader are you? This is not a judgmental question, but just a question to cajole your awareness, to get you back on track, to orient or reorient your direction. If you understand the weight of this question, and live it in practice, it can change the world around you.

What kind of leader are you? Have you taken an honest assessment of your true self, looking and exploring deeply in the mirror of awareness? Doing so helps you understand and accept your imperfections and your unique brand of genius. Knowing where your weaknesses are reflects your humanity and allows you to embrace the imperfections in others and, in turn, to see their humanity. When you know your story and theirs, both are impossible to hate. When you know who you are, you then create the trustable ground that goes with you everywhere.

What kind of leader are you? Do you know what your purpose is? Do you live from the heart of this purpose and speak the truth of your purpose? When was the last time you used your purpose to help guide your organization, say, through crisis or change? Knowing your purpose can overcome nearly any obstacle. Knowing how to lead with heart while still keeping your head creates harmony and integrity in your world.

Do you know the difference between perception and reality? Are you aligned with the truth so you can work with the forces of the truth? When was the last time you closely examined the truth—the *why* behind *what* you do—in your work, your business, or your life? Knowing this truth, which is your *true essence* of your purpose, will become a beacon that drives you and your team through the toughest of times. Knowing this truth will both set you apart from others who might compare you and act as a magnet to those who see your truth, too.

An example of this is a real estate company I've worked with that knows the truth that it's really in the *helping residents thrive* business. This one-hundred-year-old company has reinvented itself multiple times throughout its business journey. When they evolved into the real estate company they currently are, they examined closely the business they were really getting into. You see, to them, real estate isn't just land holding, residential community development, property maintenance, or selling leases. To them, the business is really there to create vibrant livable communities where people thrive in their life. This comes to fruition through their artfully planned communities, their exceptional maintenance services, the care for knowing the families that live in their communities, and the care for their quality of life for all involved. All of this stems from the values that are inherited from their founders: to care for the quality of life of the people in their community, the nurturing of the people that contribute to the company's success, and the flourishing of their entire stakeholder lifestyle.

Here's another example.

I recently worked with the founder and leadership team of a financial products and services company who, throughout their twenty-two years in business, had never explored the depth of their *why*. At the onset of our brand evolution process, we discovered that at a young age the founder was diagnosed with a rare form of bone cancer. After a long and thankfully successful battle with cancer that devastated the family finances and bankrupted the family business, the founder committed himself to helping people, including families and small businesses, to financial health and literacy. This unique experience encouraged him to understand the depth of how financial stability makes for a safer and healthier family. His entire career has been motivated by a desire to heal the financial foundations that sit at the heart of all families and small businesses, especially family-run businesses. This discovered truth helped this leader and his leadership team more fully commit to a greater why behind his business.

This truth, when closely examined, becomes evident when you realize the essence of the business you're really in. Once discovered, this truth turns into a potent energy that fuels the business forward.

What kind of leader are you? Do you know the essence, the truth, the driving *why* behind what you do in business? Have you closely examined your core motivations as a leader? Have you asked those around you, especially the other leaders around you, what their driving motivations are? When you explore and discover the essence of your driving motivations behind your business and bring them forward through an actionable path, you reorient your trajectory as a business and as a business leader. Your *why* is the lifeblood that will propel your business through its darkest days and will be the creator for a brighter future for all involved.

What kind of leader are you? Do you notice the difference between when you're on your noble path and when you've wandered? When you wander off your path, do you know what to do to get back on it? Wandering or getting off your purpose path is fine. It will happen. You simply have to recognize it when it happens and get back on your path.

What kind of leader are you? Do you work with the reality that's in front of you and employ your mastery kit-of-parts to their highest and noblest pursuits? Have you mastered the tools of self-aware leadership? Have you applied this mastery to your greatest and highest good and the good of those you aim to serve? Knowing and being truthful—to yourself and others—about your reality and leveraging all seen and unseen forces to realize your purpose is a big step into awakened leadership.

Do you know how to lead with heart and not just your strategic mind? Are you tapped into your own intrinsic motivations and the intrinsic motivations of your team? Is your team courageously aligned at the heart, or are they working with their mind only? Are you courageous enough to embrace and claim the gift of life you've been given and apply this gift to a greater good? Are you and your team fiercely working to realize your potential? When you and your team are fully aligned and fiercely working to realize your potential, you become an insurmountable collective.

Can you see that you've awakened to greater possibilities? Are you clear on what those possibilities are, and are you convicted to making them happen? When awakened leaders live in the world of possibilities, we work with the forces of beauty. Belonging, harmony, and magnetism—each are attractive in their own way, each have their own power for the awakened leader and the beautiful business.

Can you see the impact that your leadership has on those around you? What you put out into the world is reflected back. Are you leading with love or fear? Are you making decisions with love or fear? Are you fostering love or fear in your team and organization? They feel the difference, even if they're not aware of it.

If you're on the journey to evolved leadership, you may have experienced an emergence of awareness that comes at you from the peripherals—a new horizon at which you are pointed or a rumbling that gathers from the far-off distance. During this unfolding, you get a glimpse of something that captures your curiosity—and you're called to explore it. You get an inclination that there's something more, somewhere out there. Maybe there's a quiet inner voice that you begin to hear.

To be sure, evolving leadership, like all forms of artistry, is a process and a practice, not a destination. The artistry of it requires you, the leader, to claim this path. And it is an invitation. An invitation to go beyond top-down, command-and-control leadership into a form of integrated leadership living.

Once you're aware of what kind of leader you are and the information that people are delivering to you and receiving from you, your entire worldview shifts. When you see what others reflect back to you, you know what kind of leader you are. When you know what kind of leader you are, you know the effects of your motivations, words, and actions. And this becomes contagious in your team. Like attracts like. When you become a beacon for your purpose, you attract others who are called to fuse with your purpose and collectively deliver on it.

There's nothing more powerful than a group of people united through their hearts pulling together in a common cause. Awakened leaders create the circumstances for this beauty to take shape and move the world.

❝ It seems that nature— or if you will, the process of evolution— has endowed every living being with the wish to live, and whatever he believes to be his reasons are only secondary thoughts by which he rationalizes this biologically given impulse.

— ERIC FROMM, *THE ART OF BEING*

> **But yield who will to their separation,**
>
> **My object in living is to unite**
>
> **My avocation and my vocation**
>
> **As my two eyes make one in sight.**
>
> **Only where love and need are one,**
>
> **And the work is play for mortal stakes,**
>
> **Is the deed ever really done**
>
> **For heaven and the future's sakes.**

— ROBERT FROST, "TWO TRAMPS IN MUD TIME"

The Evolution of Your Beautiful Business

> **❝A person suffers if he or she is constantly being forced into the statistical mentality and away from the road of feeling.**
>
> — ROBERT BLY

Since migrating from the east coast in the early '90s, I've lived in San Diego. Famous for its great weather, the climate here is beautiful because it's essentially a desert on the ocean. The unique geographic characteristics of San Diego county boasts wildly diverse flora and fauna. As an outdoor enthusiast, normal activity for me includes trail running, surfing, hiking in local canyons, or beekeeping my hives behind our canyon home. More diverse plant life can be found here than in any other county in the US. From oceans to chaparrals to deserts to high deserts and to mountains that reach more than ten thousand feet, the diverse climate attracts diverse life. One regional phenomenon is the burst of desert wildflowers and cactus blooms that take place each spring. The best month for viewing the flora of Anza Borrego tends to be March, and especially after a very wet winter.

At the same time, when the wildflowers are blooming, the painted lady butterfly life cycle is showing itself. At their peak season, these butterflies are abundant and show up by the millions in our area, creating a visual spectacle sometimes resembling snow flurries that flutter across wide landscapes. While the painted lady is relatively common in other parts of the world, the temperate climate of Southern California is a fertile territory for this beautiful pollinator.

There are four seemingly miraculous stages to the metamorphosis of all butterflies, not just the painted lady. These stages are the egg-laying stage, the larval stage, the pupal or chrysalis stage, and the adult butterfly stages.

After roaming around on its many earth-bound legs and gorging itself on a plant-host, the painted lady caterpillar makes a simple silk pad affixing itself on the underside of a branch or twig. It twists around, embedding itself firmly in the silk cocoon. Then it sheds its skin, revealing the chrysalis. The chrysalis hangs upside down until the butterfly is ready to emerge. This complete process is called *holometabolism*, meaning "complete transformation."

During this magnificent process, there is a vital and delicate stage when the mainly undifferentiated cells turn into a milkshake-like pulp, where it reconfigures itself into the future-state butterfly. While much of the body breaks itself down, a few parts of the body, such as the legs, are more or less unchanged in this process. This pulp stage is akin to a liminal state—a state that sits between what once was and what is yet to be. Here is a vulnerable and creative time. The imaginal cells within the cocoon have nearly endless possibilities, much like stem cells.

When businesses go through an evolution, the same stages take effect. The liminal space that takes place in an evolution is the place when your business sits between the uncertain world of "formerly" or "used to be" and the aspirational space of "we're becoming" or "we want to be." Evolution at its heart resets the mindset and expectations into a place of newly designed destiny. When everything you know about your business or market changes, then it's time to review who you are and what future you're now focused on creating.

> **" Your beliefs become your thoughts,**
>
> **Your thoughts become your words,**
>
> **Your words become your actions,**
>
> **Your actions become your habits,**
>
> **Your habits become your values,**
>
> **Your values become your destiny.**
>
> — MAHATMA GANDHI

Owning Your Evolution

In order to create a beautiful business, it's likely your business needs to evolve. Evolution is a natural part of the human trajectory. As I shared in the spiral evolution graphic earlier in the book, we often have to evolve into beauty. We can't force this type of evolution with will alone. This type of unconscious growth often directs us into outward growth measurements like power, profit, and size. Beauty must be accommodated. Beauty must be allowed to take shape. Beauty requires presence and patience. We must make room for evolution into beauty to allow effective gestation of meaningful growth directions.

Meaningful change begins with an inward journey. Like the caterpillar that cocoons itself and turns to chrysalis, which evolves to butterfly, leaders awaken to the possibilities within their business by going within their own beliefs and harvesting its potential. Evolution is a remarkable human quality that allows us to thrive. Without evolution, we stand still, wither, and dissolve. Or we become extinct.

Deliberate evolution starts within. And it is sometimes in response to some external force that pushes you outside of your comfort zone and tests your character, beliefs, and commitments. Evolution is an outcome of awakening, which begins with your leadership journey. The process of evolution includes the examination of your goals, beliefs, and behaviors that drive your outcomes. The little and big things you do are what generates your results. What you believe comes from what's important to you. What you do is born from what you believe. What you do consistently generates your results. Simply said, you get what you focus on.

Your inner narrative defines what you focus on and how you see the world. This narrative is shaped by your conscious awareness. If you see the world as a threatening place, you approach it with fear. If you see the world as a competitive place, you approach it to win. If you see the world as a connective place, you approach it with cooperation. If you see the world as a creative place, you approach it with wonder. Whether you're conscious of it or not, your beliefs define your narrative, which drives your actions.

Brand as Character

As I wrote in chapter 4, self-awareness is a key cornerstone to the path of shaping leadership that creates a beautiful business. When we are self-aware as individuals, we're aware of our internal guidance system of beliefs, values, passions, and purpose, and we're aware how our behaviors affect those around us. The same is true for a business that is self-aware. And when a business has this kind of awareness, it can be highly intentional about how it expresses itself and how it relates to the world. Another word for this belief-oriented self-awareness is character. When we are aware of the attributes that define, differentiate, and distinguish ourselves, we have integrity of character. We walk our talk. We make decisions by our values and principles. We know what we believe, who we are, and how we affect others in our world.

In its simplest terms, our brand is our character, and our character is our brand. Allow me to give you a little bit of background. The origin of the words *character* can be traced back to the Greek *charassein*, meaning "to sharpen, cut in furrows, or engrave." This word gave way to the Greek word *charaktēr*, a noun meaning "mark, distinctive quality." This shared meaning is the Latin word *character*. The word *brand* comes from a fusion of the Old English word *brond*, meaning "fire, flame, destruction by fire; firebrand, piece of burning wood, torch," and (poetic) "sword," from proto-Germanic *brandaz*, meaning "a burning."

These roots of *brand* essentially amount to an "iron instrument for branding," which means "mark made by a hot iron." More modern adoptions of the word brand mean "a class of goods identified by name as the product of a single firm or manufacturer" and a "a public image, reputation, or identity conceived of as something to be marketed or promoted." However, in order to make that indelible mark, impression, and reputation, a brand has to come from something.

The word *character* comes from the Greek word *charassein*, meaning "a chisel or marketing instrument or stone or metal." As we go about living our lives through conscious or unconscious value systems, we chisel the essence of our character through our beliefs and actions of life. We chisel our way through the world, making impressions on each and every one we come into contact with. One conversation at a time, one action at a time, one moral decision at a time. Our character is the essence of who we are and how the world experiences us. This unique mark of character exists both within us, through our belief-drivers, and all around us as we leave our marks on the world. Over time, our branded character becomes our imprint, our reputation, and our legacy.

One impression at a time, as leaders we are creators of culture based on our character. Leading and building a brand with character means to create consciously and intentionally a sphere of influence where our values and beliefs, including ethics and morality, are celebrated and highlighted.

All of our actions, words, gestures, attitudes, and decisions form an impression, regardless of how big or small, which shapes both our character and the indelible impression on the world around us.

Think of the people who've had the greatest influence on your life and your character, including but not limited to your parents, your family, your teachers, your coaches, authors of influential books you've read, leaders of the faith you follow, and on and on. Each has had some influence on your character and, by extension as a leader, your company brand. How Oprah was raised affected her unique brand. How Bill Gates, Steve Jobs, Henry Ford, Martin Luther King Jr., and Abraham Lincoln were each influenced by the people and decisions that formed their character had big effects on the impact they've made in the world. Being wide-eyed about what forms your brand is the first step in making conscious efforts to cultivate the brand you want.

How the people associated with your business experience you and your team is the culmination of character attributes, which are in part driven by the moral and ethical belief systems that drive your actions. For instance, if a business carries a fixed mindset, it will drag its old self-image into the brave new future and struggle for relevance, unable to make a meaningful contribution to a waiting, wanting, and exponentially evolving world. When a business adopts a growth mindset, its character evolves, too.

The Question

I have a question I've asked in countless business meetings that, because of my work as a brand strategist, tends to start as a brand-orienting question but at its heart is really a business trajectory question. From my perspective it is the single most powerful question in business and one which, if answered clearly, will create value for your customers, inspire your team, get your company through good times and bad, make or break a business, and, if it's audacious enough, might just change the world.

In truth, it's really a two-part question. Here's the question in its varied forms: **Beyond making money, why does your company exist? Stated differently, for what reason does your company deserve to be in business? What value does your company and its products or services offer the world? Stated soberly, because launching and running a business is very hard work and not for the faint of heart, aside from money alone, why does your business exist and what's in it for your customer?**

If you can't answer this question with clarity and you don't have the inclination to do so, you're likely doing it for the money and, most likely, for the money alone. There's nothing inherently wrong with doing something for the money alone, especially if you're in survival mode. However, if the state of your business is not in survival mode, unfortunately you might be squandering a huge opportunity to offer the world something more valuable than the profit you keep. I can say with some conviction that the world doesn't need yet another company who's in it just for the money.

Just as people cannot live without eating, so a business cannot live without profits. But most people don't live to eat, and neither must businesses live just to make profits.

—JOHN MACKEY AND RAJ SISODIA, *CONSCIOUS CAPITALISM*

While doing it for the money alone may be enough for some people, most good, well-meaning, and thoughtful business leaders will eventually evolve to ask themselves one of the most challenging questions in life and business, a question that some are not courageous enough to rigorously investigate: Why does your company exist?

❝ Economics that hurt the moral well-being of an individual or a nation are immoral and, therefore, sinful.

— MAHATMA GANDHI

Good News, Bad News

If you can't answer the above question, I've got bad news and good news for you.

The bad news is, you've founded or are operating your company without the clarity of a true north, compass, or rudder. When faced with your most critical business decisions, are you yielding to the one that makes the most profit, which is sometimes at odds with that which is best for your people or your customers and beyond? If so, your company has yet to define your purpose. You haven't yet clearly articulated your reason for being that can help you navigate through the forces that are beyond your control. And you may be lost, floating aimlessly in a sea of dollars, cents, and market forces, and you may not know it. However, this is another way to consider doing business.

The good news is that if you have an inclination to answer the question or curiosity to discover your company's essential reason for being, then this book will help you answer it and put it into amplified action.

It's also likely, if you have an inclination to answer the question, that your company is in it for more than just the money and that your purpose is there, somewhere within layers of people, products and/or services, complexity, and processes. It's likely there with a faint but steadily present heartbeat. And this book can help you discover your purpose, put it to work for your company, and infuse it into your brand, your culture, and your business.

I've asked the above question countless times at the onset of business relationships, and more times than not the question is met with a bewildered look of puzzled delight. A combination of confusion mixed with wonder or curiosity, with a dash of "yes, of course" thrown in. Eye contact either deepens eye-to-eye with a sense of curiosity, strays upward in curious search for a clear answer, or is downcast with a hint of bewilderment.

The body language tends to be alert, with a lean-in posture, or some people are thrown back in their seat. The confusion typically comes because most business leaders haven't asked themselves or ever fully considered the question. The wonder is the childlike delight and invitation to consider something that on one level is relatively abstract and on the other level grounded in a deep realism and a vast realm of meaningful possibilities for them and their business. The "yes, of course" comes from the near-immediate awareness that this question is such a profoundly basic yet vital question to ask and answer that most businesses at their onset skip over it for its seemingly apparent *obviousness*.

To be both fair and honest, answering the question is not easy for most leaders. And it is harder still to put into simple, actionable language that ignites the passion and imagination of teams and customers. It's a hard question to answer because it sits at the foundation of all a business has done, all it has become, and all it is becoming. Answering it requires a sifting, sorting, and surveying of the business's internal landscape that dwells deep into the heart of why it is here on this planet. It's also hard to answer for ourselves because our perspective on our beliefs is often muddled with the complexity of living. We're really close to ourselves. And our self-awareness can be clouded with the busyness of life.

I have deep respect for good business
leaders. It's been my experience that the
vast majority of business leaders that I've
worked with are intelligent, hardworking,
thoughtful, skilled, caring, experienced,
and disciplined people, who care
passionately and work diligently to make
their business succeed and offer value to
their customers.

As well, many business leaders also have a high level of
emotional intelligence, with deep care for their business,
their family, their employees, and their customers. Many
know how to lead people with respect and integrity.
Many of the strongest leaders have the ability to lean into
empathy to see the world of others and to see their world
as it could be without deceiving themselves as to the
current realities of their business, product, or market.

And I've also worked with my fair share of short-sighted,
ill-tempered, unethical, thoughtless, mean, maniacal, and
downright disrespectful managers. I hesitate calling them
leaders. I've been burned by some, stolen from, embezzled
from, lied to, stiffed with nonpayment, and have fired
companies and people because of these behaviors. I've
got an advanced degree from the business school of hard
knocks and have learned from some of the best, brightest,
and most caring people any of us could hope to learn from
in our lives. For all of this hard-knock experience, I'm thankful,
because the pain has led me to my deep desire: my own
personal purpose to help leaders arrive at the question "Why
does your company exist?" and the experience to help them
artfully and authentically determine their answer and move
that answer into conscious action.

> **❝ An exchange of empathy provides an entry point for a lot of people to see what healing feels like.**
>
> — TARANA BURKE

Indirect Pursuit of Your *Why*

While the question that I ask is ultimately a *why*-oriented question (e.g., Why does your business exist beyond making money?), and an important one to answer, I've learned that I can't come at this question directly and expect people to have an answer unless they've already done the exploration work to answer it clearly. The challenge is that why-oriented questions tend to escape our conscious awareness because of our unconscious drivers. Simply said, your *whats* tend to uncover your *why*. Your foundational why usually only reveals itself through time, practice, and examination. Let me explain.

If I were to ask you why you founded your business, you might respond to me with a list of circumstances and actions that encouraged that decision. You might tell me that you were laid off from your senior level position and needed to make a living. "To make a living" is your why here. Or you might say you had an idea for a product you could produce or a service you could provide that was both valuable and you didn't see anyone else offering to customers. Your why here is that you saw a need and provided a solution to fill it.

For me, why I started my business was really a chain of whats. When my wife and I moved to California, it was because I was completely burning out from working in Washington, DC, working nearly seven days a week for an unethical person that I no longer wanted to work for. When we moved here, I asked myself, what can I do now that will remedy my burnout and still allow me to make a good living? What have I learned about my craft that I can apply to others who need my expertise? What skills, tools, and insights do I have that are valuable to others? None of these questions get at the why behind my series of whats. In other words, what drove me to start my business doesn't really get me any closer to my why. At least not at first.

There are a series of tools I've developed over time and borrowed from others that might help you pursue your why. Go to www.the-beautiful-business.com to download this tool kit.

What *Why* Can Do for Us All

In our consumer markets, there is the constant need to push, promote, and produce more products of lesser quality that fill garages, closets, storage units, and landfills. According to Statista, the average size home in 2019 was twenty-five hundred square feet, nearly doubling from 1975, when homes averaged sixteen hundred square feet.[30] Meanwhile, the US Census numbers measured that average household family size has dropped from 3.33 household members in 1960 to 2.52 in 2019.[31] While there are, on average, less household members per home, we now seem to require more real estate for the growing amount of stuff we own.

Some advertising agencies, who make their primary living off of media buying and planning, would have us believe that if we do not keep up with the latest gadgets, the newest car, the latest fashion, and the biggest house, we are not keeping up with the status quo. As Dr. Martin Luther King reminds us, "One of the great liabilities of history is that all too many people fail to remain awake through great periods of social change. Every society has its protectors of status quo and its fraternities of the indifferent who are notorious for sleeping through revolutions. Today, our very survival depends on our ability to stay awake, to adjust to new ideas, to remain vigilant and to face the challenge of change."[32]

A beautiful business takes us outside the superficial into the profound, past the collection of things into the realm of connection, beyond fragmentation into belonging, past the ordinary into the extraordinary, beyond transactions into transcendent experiences.

In the day-to-day life of striving for more, more, more, we seem to have forgotten the beauty that comes from simplicity. It seems to me that overdone consumerism, social media curation of perfect moments, and the near-constant attention we give to our many screens (smartphones, computers, TV, and the like) have overtaken our attention of what matters most. We seem so busy keeping up with the Joneses that we've lost sight of the underlying "why it all matters."

And with the tribalism that exists within our political environment, and some segments of our Western culture, we seem to have lost sight that we humans have more in common than we have in differentiation. We have lost sight of the things that matter most in life. The top five regrets of the dying, as shared by Palliative Nurse Bonnie Ware, are:

- I'd wish I'd had the courage to live a life true to myself.
- I wish I hadn't worked so hard.
- I wish I'd had the courage to express my feelings.
- I wish I had stayed in touch with my friends.
- I wish that I had let myself be happier.

I read this between the lines of the top five regrets of the dying:

- Put people and relationships ahead of work.
- Embrace the courage to be yourself, which requires enough self-awareness to know yourself.
- Tend to the things that really matter—nurturing relationships, being true to yourself, expressing your feelings, and allowing yourself to be happy and fulfilled.

There's a scene in *Dead Poets Society* where professor John Keating, an inspiring and provocative English teacher at a private boy's school, leads the boys out of their classroom into a hallway lined with trophy cases filled with photos of past students. "Seize the day," he urges them. "Because, believe it or not, each and every one of us in this room is one day going to stop breathing, turn cold, and die."[33] In the hallway where Mr. Keating is lecturing, he encourages the boys to take a close look into the eyes of these past students, many of them long dead. "If you listen real close, you can hear them whisper their legacy to you. Go on, lean in. Listen. You hear it? 'Carpe . . .' You hear it? 'Carpe . . . Carpe diem. Seize the day, boys. Make your lives extraordinary.'" Some of Mr. Keating's teachings are centered on the words of Walt Whitman: "The powerful play goes on, and you may contribute a verse." My business is part of this play. Your business is part of this play. The character your business presents in the play of life can be anything of your choosing. Your role as a leader is part of this play of life, and we get to choose the intention, setting, purpose, and application of our contributions to life.

Calling the Better Angels of Our Nature

We've lost sight of the primal truth that we humans are inextricably connected to one another, to all living things, and to the beautiful planet we call home. And that is we the people who decide, through our thoughts and feelings, and define, through our actions, what our societies and cultures are made of. It is up to us to vindicate a confidence in the goodness of society that's built upon a capitalistic economy in the face of so much manifest wrongdoing within it. Our course correction lies within our ability to manifest the inherent goodness that is embedded within all of us. This is what Abraham Lincoln referred to in his first inaugural address: "the better angels of our nature." What is most missing from much of our highly technological world and the separatism in our society are the three core attributes that define the beautiful business: belonging, harmony, and magnetism.

While our Western culture is partially built on a healthy and thriving economy, part of the beauty of living in a democratic republic is that a capitalist society gives me the permission to make a living and a life as I see fit. Call it the pursuit of happiness or the search for personal liberty: these permissions are woven into the fabric of our culture. While our capitalist playing field makes any number of pursuits possible, there's mounting data to suggest that ever bigger houses and more things don't necessarily make us happier. "As we amass more and more possessions, we don't get any happier—we simply raise our reference point," researcher James Roberts, of the Hankamer School of Business at Baylor University, stated. "That new twenty-five-hundred-square-foot house becomes the baseline for your desires for an even bigger house. It's called the Treadmill of Consumption. We continue to purchase more and more stuff but we don't get any closer to happiness, we simply speed up the treadmill."[34]

One CEO I was advising confessed to me that the treadmill of profit, growth, and materialism was crushing him. "I chase and chase and chase, with no end in sight. I feel this heavy burden each and every day," he admitted. He'd achieved what most people would call a highly successful career; well known in his industry, a seven-figure compensation package, multiple homes, fancy suits and sport cars, and enough stock value to not think twice about buying even more. The cost of the treadmill for this CEO, then at the age of fifty-one, was two divorces, five children that barely speak to him, and health issues including a heart stint, high blood pressure, and diabetes. All of this was measured in the circle of colleagues that are constantly comparing their collection of homes, cars, boats, and more.

"What's the point?" he asked. "I end up working so hard that when I do have time away, I no longer have people close to share it with in a meaningful way. They say, 'it's lonely at the top,' and this is not just for leaders or CEOs; it's lonely for people who spend most of their time working only to find themselves isolated in their life. I'm lonely. And that needs to change; and the only way I think I can change that is to get back to what matters most to me. I've lost my way and I want to rediscover it."

Many of us don't need more stuff; we need more meaning. Meaning is what fulfills us. Self-awareness is the playing field of meaning. Purpose is the threshold to meaning. And it's meaning that people seek. Employees seek it in their work, and customers seek it in how they spend their hard-earned money. All of this meaning-seeking gets to the heart of why our "why" matters. The why in your business is called your brand's purpose. In knowing your why and activating it in your company, it will become your true north in guiding you to a business creation that is both true to itself and positively impacts the world.

Why Brand Purpose Matters

> **❝ Work and life are not separate things and therefore cannot be balanced against each other except to create further trouble.**
>
> — DAVID WHYTE, *THE THREE MARRIAGES: REIMAGINING WORK, SELF AND RELATIONSHIP*

During a conversation with a client partner, the CEO asked this question: "Why does brand purpose matter to anyone inside or outside the organization?"

At first, I was a little surprised by the question. My mistake was working with the assumption that, by now, most business leaders understand the value and impact of an activated purpose. Allow me to correct that mistake and shed some light on the question.

Many business leaders and entrepreneurs, especially if they are the founder of a business, rely on their passion to be automatically understood and replicated by their staff and understood by their customers. Their passion runs deep, but that may not be the case for others. Of course, their driving passion in itself can be contagious if it's authentic. We see this in charismatic leaders.

Speaking honestly, much of their staff may be working just to earn a living and have a decent job, at least in the beginning. As such, there is often a void of untapped energy being missed by keeping this passion locked up inside a founder or a core leadership team.

A defined and activated why that gets entrepreneurs and team members going above and beyond just collecting a paycheck can become a force for change in the organization and elsewhere. When this why is defined, written down, and put into action throughout the organization, it exponentially enlarges its impact.

Consider this: what might start off as an individual's purpose—for a founder, CEO, or any leader—can be catalyzed into a "brand purpose."

"In the hands of a mature, healthy human being—one who has achieved full humanness—power . . . is a great blessing. But in the hands of the immature, vicious, or emotionally sick, power is a horrible danger.

— ABRAHAM MASLOW

CHAPTER 8

The Psychology of Branded-Business

I'm going to let you in on a secret in my work. I see nearly all brand and culture attributes of a business in psychological terms. As modern business is an evolved invention of humans, we have made it in our likeness. I see the work of business through psychological lenses because most of the hard parts of work are what are referred to as the soft skills—the human-to-human attributes of business.

As the saying credited to Peter Drucker goes, "culture eats strategy for breakfast." I believe a healthy culture is your best strategy. Your people create your innovative products, they care for your customers, they build the systems and processes to produce the work, they align together in collaboration for the work, they activate your marketing, and they lead in cohesion with your organization's values. As I've stated already and it bears reinforcing, I believe your brand is your character, and your character is your brand. The actions that are driven by the living beliefs of the people within your organization make up the indelible impression they create on the world and one another.

—

In my undergraduate studies, I earned a minor in psychology. I learned just enough about the psych world to realize I didn't want to be a psychologist for a living. However, I was able to apply it to my life and work and begin to understand how great minds like Carl Jung, B. F. Skinner, Jean Piaget, Erik Erikson, Abraham Maslow, and William James thought, studied, and positively impacted our adventures in the human psyche.

Among my greatest influences in the psychological world was Carl Jung, for his studies of archetypes that build on the thinking of other great minds such as Immanuel Kant's categories, Plato's Ideas, and Schopenhauer's prototype. In fact, I use Jung's twelve primary archetypes in processes I lead brand leader's through in helping them identify the driving archetype for their business, so they can embody it when living the brand.

If business is worth doing, it's worth doing remarkably well, with clear intent of the characteristics that unify and differentiate my business and while offering real value to the world of my customers. After all, creating value is really the only reason a business should exist. And in order to be remarkable in my work, I feel I need to strive to serve something greater than myself. In order to become a remarkable business and brand, I must serve a greater good. I must, in some way, serve the world. Even if the world, as I define it, is the audience at which I aim my business.

In Abraham Maslow's original Hierarchy of Needs, self-actualization sat atop the five need levels within his well-known model created in the mid-1940s. It's often represented as a pyramid, but Maslow didn't express it this way. The shortcomings of how most people see this misrepresented pyramid is that once you've achieved the foundational level, you move up levels of the pyramid. Life, work, and business doesn't work this way. As I stated earlier, evolving toward a beautiful business is a way of being in business, not a final destination. Maslow's now-famous model suggests that by having met a reasonable degree of your physiological needs, such as safety, love and belonging, and esteem, you can ultimately arrive at this realm where "what a man *can* be, he *must* be."[35] To be clear, he was talking about women, too.

In this realm, Maslow presented that a person must strive for and achieve what she or he is—as my Irish friends say, "able for"—and driven to be. This need to create and become everything we can be—an accomplished entrepreneur, chef, gardener, scientist, parent, or artist—is the height of human existence. Here, Maslow suggests that when we strive to do what we are called to, do what we love, apply our natural genius, gifts, talents, and opportunities, we become self-actualized.

Maslow was talking about more than the simple and often overstated mantra of just "follow your passion." Or as Joseph Campbell put it, "follow your bliss." Both were saying that one must completely apply themselves to all their gifts, passions, and opportunities to become self-actualized.

66 Musicians must make music, artists must paint, poets must write if they are to be ultimately at peace with themselves. What human beings can be, they must be. They must be true to their own nature. This need we may call self-actualization . . . It refers to man's desire for self-fulfillment, namely to the tendency for him to become actually in what he is potentially.

— ABRAHAM MASLOW, *MOTIVATION AND PERSONALITY*

It's not well known, but Maslow amended his hierarchy-of-needs model in his later years. This revised model offered eight stages of human developmental needs, each with its own unique attributes, which build on one another and act as thresholds to the next.

Again, I tend to see a business metaphorically, like a human: the systems and process of the business are like the biology of a body, and the thoughts and beliefs that drive behavior are the psychological aspects of the business. As businesses are created, evolved, and matured, the people within them create this maturation. No business evolves on its own without the people within shaping, molding, guiding, and nurturing it forward. All of the attributes of Maslow's needs outlined below are applicable both on the individual and cultural levels. So as you read through the following list of needs, think about how each applies to where you are as an individual and leader and where your team is in relation to this model.

Here are the eight Maslow needs, explained.

1. **Biological needs:** In this stage, we seek basic animal needs, including food, warmth, shelter, sex, water, and other bodily needs. When someone goes into "survival mode," they go into ensuring they have the basics they need to survive. If someone is thirsty or hungry or their body is physiologically or chemically unbalanced, all of their resources will turn toward curing these shortages, and subsequent needs remain dormant. As such, if their basic biological needs are not met, they would never be able to trust their surroundings and would be stuck in a place of survival anxiety, unable to move beyond.

   For a business, this might translate into the need for funding, capital, profit, systems, or processes. At the core of this is enough financial, time, and energetic resources to ensure the business operates in a healthy and sustainable manner.

2. **Safety needs:** These needs have to do with one's desire and search for a secure, orderly, and predictable environment in which the familiar is frequent, life is relatively predictable, and inconsistency and injustice are minimized. With their biological needs reasonably fulfilled, the individual's safety needs take over and dominate their focus and drive to fulfill. The need for predictability and consistency, if not satisfied, leads to feelings of fear, distrust, and shame instead of feelings of control, autonomy, and predictability. When we have a sense of safety within our environment, we can then move on to higher need levels.

   For a company, this need for safety includes team psychological safety, such as the ability to trust one another or to not feel threatened at work. Some predictability in how people treat one another—or a sense of job safety—applies here.

3. **Belonging needs:** Once one's biological and safety needs are gratified, the third layer of one's needs are social. Here Maslow points to the social-psychological aspects of needs including emotionally based relationships. This includes friendship, sexual intimacy, and having a supportive and communicative family. If one does not experience close relationships, one experiences negative social connection, which manifests in shame, guilt, disconnection, and disorientation.

   Our sense of belonging in the workplace defines and secures who we are in the culture, how we belong to the team, and the degree to which we are accepted and embraced for who we are.

4. **Self-esteem needs:** Attaining self-esteem, self-respect, and respect for others are needs that all humans have. In this stage, one needs to engage with the world, express themselves, and have practices that give a person a sense of contribution. Unsatisfied, this leads to feelings of worthlessness or inferiority. Feelings of inferiority in turn may lead to low agreeableness, disengagement, or futility.

   We begin to understand the value we provide in our vocation, and the world responds positively. This creates a feedback loop of self-awareness and self-value. This contribution could be gratitude expressed for a job well done or a position advancement with more responsibility. Regardless, the more impact someone realizes they have, the more esteem that's created. This is why feedback and recognition is so vital in cultural life.

5. **Cognitive needs:** Cognitive needs are the natural human need to explore, discover, learn, and create in order to gain insight for a clearer understanding of the world. Maslow believed that humans have the need for intellectual growth, exploration, and expansion of their knowledge. When unfulfilled, this need for intellectual growth leads to confusion, stagnation, or an identity crisis.

   In the workplace, this is directly related to the need to explore, experiment, and be open to new and unpredictable experiences. Innovative collaboration in teams plays a role in fostering our cognitive needs. By stretching our intellectual limits and exploring new experiences, we feel more alive and vital. This meets the paradox of curiosity: we feel most safe when things are predictable, but most alive when they are not.

6. **Aesthetic needs:** Maslow believed that humans need beauty in a variety of forms in order to continue the journey to self-actualization. In this stage, humans need to rejuvenate themselves in the presence and beauty of nature and in elements that reflect the beauty of nature, all while immersing in, absorbing, and observing their surroundings.

   In our work, this is why environment and design are so important. By working in a beautiful environment that is felt, not just seen, we are enlivened by wonder and awe. This higher need cultivates a deep connection with feelings of intimacy, wonder, and awe to our work and with our colleagues.

7. **Self-actualization needs:** This need sat atop Maslow's original hierarchy and speaks to the stage where one experiences their own self-mastery and applies it to their life and work. Self-actualization is the intuitive need of humans to make the most of their abilities and strive to be the best they can, building on all previous needs.

   When we fulfill our self-actualization in our work, we cultivate feelings of creativity, purposefulness, and healthy gratification. Here, we go beyond measuring ourselves on compensation, and we shift our measurement focus to the degree of positive impact or change we're making through our work. This turns into an intrinsic reward loop.

8. **Self-transcendence needs:** Finally, in his later years, Maslow divided the top of the hierarchy to add self-transcendence, which has also been referred to as spiritual needs. This is the need that goes beyond the self, where an altruistic and intrinsic application of all of our humanity is applied

to benefit the world. One's spiritual needs are unique in that they can be accessed at any *need* stage in one's journey.

When this need is fulfilled in our work and our life, we transcend into feelings of wholeheartedness, purpose, harmony, and spiritual connection.

In this highest calling of self-transcendence, an individual finds themselves called to transcend beyond the self to an altruistic goal outside of one's self. This purpose for being, living, and working, while self-prescribed and chosen freely, goes far beyond what one can create for oneself. Instead, the viewpoint of purpose goes beyond the individual and into the world around.

In this newer highest arena, we are still called to be our best, do what we love (are driven to do), and achieve what we can but, in addition, give our talents, genius, gifts, and creations as an offering to the world. Here, we live, love, and work in the intersection between human creation and service to humankind. Rather than being driven solely by wealth or status, we choose an ambitious and meaningful life and vocation purpose.

Transcendent Business Experiences

Moreover, as our life and businesses increasingly become designed around the need to self-actualize, then self-transcend, Maslow reveals that we become more inclined to "peak experiences." The opportunity for peak experiences increases as a result of the biological, psychological, emotional, and spiritual development of individuals, cultures, and society at large. Maslow proposed that the difference between "nonpeakers" and "peakers"—that is, those who prefer status quo and those who welcome transformative experiences—is the separation of two groups of people: the explorers of the depths and heights, and those who bask in the comfort of being "tranquilized by the trivial."

> **❝ Self-actualizing people have the wonderful capacity to appreciate again and again, freshly and naively, the basic goods of life, with awe, pleasure, wonder and even ecstasy, however stale these experiences may have become to others.**
>
> — ABRAHAM MASLOW, *MOTIVATION AND PERSONALITY*

In his book *Peak: How Great Companies Get Their Mojo from Maslow*, author Chip Conley explains, "This book is about the miracle of human potential: employees living up to their full potential in the workplace, customers feeling the potential bliss associated with having their unrecognized needs met, and investors feeling fulfilled by seeing the potential of their capital leveraged."[36] Conley continues:

> Maslow's message struck a chord with many business leaders. In essence, he said that with humans, there's a qualitative difference between not being sick and feeling healthy or truly alive. This idea could be applied to companies, most of which fall into the middle ground of not sick but not truly alive. Based on his Hierarchy of Needs, the solution for a company that wants to ascend up the healthy pyramid is not just to diminish the negative or to get too preoccupied with basic needs but instead to focus on aspirational needs. This idea is rather blasphemous for some. The tendency in psychology and in business has always been to focus on the deficits. Psychologists and business consultants look for what's broken and try to fix it. Yet, 'fixing it' doesn't necessarily offer the opportunity for transformation to a more optimal state of being or productivity.[37]

Maslow viewed the human journey on the path of self-actualizing much like a horticulturist, whose path was to "enable people to become healthy and effective in their own style."[38] According to Maslow, this meant that "we try to make a rose into a good rose, rather than seek to change roses into lilies." He was a passionate advocate for the need for "Being-Psychology"—a field that explores the investigation of ends rather than means. This includes end-experiences (like wonder, connection, laughter), end-values (such as beauty, truth, justice), end-goals (such as having a true north or purpose), and treating people as an end unto themselves (such as Being-Love). This field of Being-Psychology is what we call Positive Psychology today, and it's the reason that people like Martin Seligman (author of *Authentic Happiness* and coauthor of *Character Strengths and Virtues*), Mihaly Csikszentmihalyi (author of *Flow: The Psychology of Optimal Experience*), Shawn Achor (Author of *The Happiness Advantage*), and Angela Duckworth (author of *Grit*) are so well respected in business-culture circles.

Certainly, it's worth noting and reminding us that societal circumstances play a role in one's ability to reach and consistently live within Maslow's described state of self-transcendence. Some of us, like me, are lucky enough to be born holding a lottery ticket of life circumstances or standing on third base. Some are not. And, of course, life happens. Disease, a global pandemic, health issues, accidents, divorce, bankruptcy, war, and titanic economic shifts all have aftermaths. Many of these events are out of our control. These events and circumstances of life can change which zone we inhabit in Maslow's hierarchy model, and these circumstances can inhibit our ability to go to or stay in the self-transcendent zone.

This aside, assuming our fundamental human needs for food, shelter, love, belonging, and security are in place, we have some choice as to how we spend and apply our time, energy, skills, and genius. And how and why we do business.

While Maslow's perspective has been extremely influential over the past half century in the world of psychology, there is a basic truth that applies to the world of business in his foundational thinking. Like humans, businesses move through the various stages of evolution. From survival to thriving and many stages in between, businesses can reach and should strive for their own version of self-transcendence. They should ultimately ask and answer their own version of the question "How can the company best use its products or services—and how can the people within these companies use their talents, gifts and passions—to serve and benefit humankind to its fullest?"

The Value of Values

When one breaks down the definition of "value" or "values," you can quickly realize these are really two sides to a coin. Webster's dictionary definitions allude to this. The first definition of value means "the regard that something is held to deserve; the importance, worth, or usefulness of something." Here the definition of value points to the material or monetary worth of something. The term "face value" comes to mind, which means the perceived worth of something compared to the price paid or asked for it.

The next definition of value is "a person's principles or standards of behavior; one's judgment of what is important in life."

When we apply this to the world of business, it shows up like this. When I am clear about my own values or the values of my business and they show up in the consistent behaviors of my business and the people within it, it defines the qualities of the products or services we create. The qualities that define how Pixar, for instance, creates its animated stories shows up in the end result of the movies. These qualities are its values or principles. In turn, Pixar attracts movie audiences who align with these values, and that's part of the value they receive from the movies that Pixar creates. The same is true for Patagonia, Subaru, and every brand on the planet. The values that show up in the products and services of all companies attract customers with aligned values. It's worth a reminder that all business is a human-to-human connection. As consumers, we're attracted—magnetized, you might say—to the brands that we see represented in our own values. We become loyal purchasers and advocate those brands we most deeply align with on a values level. This alignment plays a significant role in value creation.

My simplest definition of marketing is the storytelling processes that articulate value to customers. My simplest definition of sales is serving or helping. When a company is practicing effective marketing, they are creating a clear communication that answers the customer-centric question, "What's in it for me?"

When a business thinks about sales, I would suggest they replace the word "selling" with either "helping" or "serving." Their sales stance at a primary level should articulate *Here's how we can help you, and here's how we can serve you.*

So the clearer you are on your values, the clearer you are on your value to customers. And, by the way, the clearer you are on your values, the clearer you should be on who your customers might be. If you work to align values, you forge deeper magnetism with your right customers.

Viewed this way, values and value become a through-line continuum from you and your team to your customers and their lives. Our values are so important because they define not only why you do but what you do and how you do it.

Brand Essence Tool

Conversely, the brand essence is a phrase that expresses the fundamental nature of a business. It goes much deeper than the industry a company competes in, such as consumer electronics, sporting goods, nonprofit, education, etc. A business leadership team or marketing team can go through a series of reflective exercises developing effective ways of expressing the brand essence by underscoring the unique value they provide.

The deeply instructive question originated by Theodore Levitt and evangelized by Peter Drucker—"What business are we in?"—can help an organization drill down on the essence of their business. Disney answered this question with *to create magic*. Airbnb's answer to this is to *democratize hospitality*. BMW's essence is *pleasure driving*. Quicksilver's is the *spirit of outdoor activity*. When a business is in what Maslow called their peak experience, they deliver on their essence, their purpose, and their promise.

Here's a tool designed to help you get to the essence of your business. This simple practice is a variation on the well-known "5X" tool in which participants are exploring the essence of something—for instance, the essence of a brand. The practice is simple yet potent. Let's assume you're doing a workshop with your leadership team. Ask each participant to write down the answer to this question five times, without repeating their answer.

Here's an example of how this exercise might go:

1. What business am I in?
   I'm in the business of evolving brands and cultures.

2. What business am I in?
   I'm in the business of connecting leadership beliefs with cultural behaviors.

3. What business am I in?
   I'm in the business of guiding leaders to a more beautiful business.

4. What business am I in?
   I'm in the business of connecting your customers to your brand purpose.

5. What business am I in?
   I'm in the business of helping leaders identify the heart and soul of their business and activating this through their culture and brand.

The Soul of the Business

Like humans, businesses can operate with a high level of consciousness. Just as humans have a soul, so can a business have a metaphorical soul. A soul in the business sense can be defined as the vital life force behind the animating activities that brings the entity to life. The soul of the brand comes from the animating power that comes from an activated purpose. While I certainly don't want to scare readers off with this idea, I do believe that there can be a *spiritual* aspect, widely defined in nonreligious terms, to business. To be clear, I am not talking about religion or god or worship. Rather, I'm talking about a collective animation that brings like-hearted people together to do what we cannot do on our own. When we fuse forces in teams, cultures, and societies that are tapping into the higher angels of our nature, we can create exponential outcomes that even the best, brightest, and most powerful individuals cannot do on their own.

This is what Brené Brown refers to as *collective effervescence*. Here, Brown is speaking to the combined human connection that is realized at the individual level and applied to our way of being in the world.

In *Braving the Wilderness*, Brené Brown speaks to some of the core philosophies outlined in her earlier work, and she provides her own definition for spirituality: "Spirituality is recognizing and celebrating that we are all inextricably connected to each other by a power greater than all of us, and that our connection to that power and to one another is grounded in love and compassion."[39]

This collective effervescence fuses us together and taps into our deep human need to belong, and it amplifies this when we pull together for a common purpose.

San Francisco is home to Hopelab. From their inception, Hopelab has been innovatively focused on the health and well-being of teens and young adults. Their first project was called "Re-Mission—a video game in which teens and young adults with cancer could virtually destroy enemy cells. It forged a deeper understanding of the link between behavioral science and physical health, showing how behavior change can improve health outcomes for young people. Study results, published in August 2008 in the peer-reviewed medical journal Pediatrics,[40] indicated that playing Re-Mission led to more consistent treatment adherence and accelerated rate of increase in cancer knowledge and self-efficacy in young cancer patients.

Since this initial and highly successful project, they've expanded their reach and built upon their foundational beliefs, working to encourage childhood physical activity, design family-strengthening tools for young mothers and their babies, and help teenagers cultivate emotion-regulating strategies and skills. Their diversity of projects and partnerships is as impressive as their impact. They believe that in order to make the greatest impact on the world, they need to align with myriad like-minded partners to scale their interventions and apply them where they are most needed. The collective effervescence of Hopelab, along with their myriad partners—including Yale Center for Emotional Intelligence, Nurse-Family Partnership, The Jed Foundation, Grit Digital Health, Well Being Trust, and Stupid Cancer—tethers close work with academic researchers, design firms, other philanthropic organizations, and even entire health-care systems to fuse behavioral psychology with socially impactful design. All of this is done with the hopes of achieving the broadest impact to teens, young adults, and families. The collective effervescence of Hopelab, their partners, and their patients is just one example of how an organization that orchestrates many and varied stakeholders leads to a potent unified force with a common drive.

Creating Magnetism through Brand Experiences

In the tiny town of Panzano, nestled in the rolling foothills of the Chianti region of Italy, resides and works a world-renowned butcher. This is no ordinary butcher.

As you walk through the charming streets of Panzano, you come upon an unignorably brilliant two-story building adorned in bold red and white stripes. This visual sensation is broken up only with the head of a carved wild boar and a deceivingly simple memorial for the proclaimed death of *bistecca florentina*. Above the entry is a sign, chiseled in marble, which reads *Antica Macelleria Cecchini*. At the same time, you're assaulted with the alluring smells of grilled delights coming from somewhere you can't quite pinpoint.

If you catch it at the right time of day, whenever the mood strikes him and there's enough audience to eat it up, you might hear the butcher's booming voice reciting—in Italian of course—long and passionately delivered passages of Dante's *Divine Comedy*. As you scan the butcher's shop, your senses are assaulted with a palette of smoked meats consisting of prosciutto, bresaola, coppa, lonza, pancetta, and pesta hanging from the ceiling. At the counters behind glass you'll see an array of meat cuts meticulously presented on finely crafted woodblocks. Red and white consume you—the walls, the marbled meats, the red shirts contrasting the white aprons of staff uniforms.

While it may not make any sense to you yet, you have been thoroughly drenched into a unique *paradisio*. This butcher's heaven is the world of Dario Cecchini. The world-renowned butcher descends from a long line—eight generations and counting. He has stoked and reinvented an antique-style *macelleria* (a.k.a. top-notch butcher) on the site of the family shop, which was destroyed during World War II.

Together, with Dario's family tradition, the business serves as a landmark and signpost of culinary, artistic, and poetic delight. It's a living homage to the high-touch craftsmanship and celebration of beauty that Italy is known for. He and the preceding generations before him have continued the lineage of a beautiful business.

Why the memorial of the death of bistecca florentina? Why Dante? Why the butcher's shop and restaurant with such a dramatic presentation?

Dario rose to notoriety during the mad cow disease crisis when eating a bistecca florentina, or massive T-bone steak, was prohibited for health reasons. He orchestrated a mock funeral, which the plaque commemorates.

As for Dante, according to Italian language scholars, his *Divinia Commedia* (*Divine Comedy*) is responsible for defining the seat of today's Italian language. Prior to the publications of his epic poem, there were multiple dialects spoken throughout Italy. The dialect in the Florence region that Dante spoke and wrote in became the accepted national language because the *Divine Comedy* was so widely read and adored. The poetic language used in Dante's epic poem, in a sense, united the language of Italy.

In Dario's macellaria, you can order nearly any cut of meticulously prepared meat imaginable, or in his restaurant you are offered a highly curated menu, including the sushi of Italy. But his family businesses are not really about meat at all. Dario is on a mission to reclaim this uniquely Italian traditional past and is pushing against large chain grocery stores. He aims to protect and promote the traditional local butcher from the rise of the powerful supermarkets who, even in Italy, are seeking to overtake smaller businesses. He believes butchery is an ancient art that involves a respect for the animal in a nearly sacred fashion, and sees his role as educator, teacher, and promoter of this tradition. The family businesses are about a tradition of craftsmanship that is at the core of the Italian lifestyle.

Dario and his macelleria empire are living evidence that one need not be a big brand—a brand centered within a thriving American metropolis, a business centered around the hypertrendy edges of culture or funded with millions of VC dollars—to be a beautiful and viable business.

Beautiful businesses are unignorable brands, which have their own gravity, their own magnetism. And Dario is certainly not alone. Brands like Southwest Airlines, Zappos, Nike, Apple, Patagonia, Tesla, and Disney are all darlings in the brand media world. Behind these huge organizations sits a slew of lesser-known companies, like Dario's, who are doing extraordinary work in the world.

Skimming through headlines and social media feeds, big brands that have their own gravity are among the most attention-getting brands. Rightly so. Many have great innovation taking place, several have remarkable cultures, and some are doing noteworthy but quiet work preferring instead to focus on creating their own gravity in their own way. Much of the stories and news reported on these brands stand in stark contrast to recently blemished brands like Volkswagen/Audi, Wells Fargo, and Uber.

Getting lots of press in big media outlets is only one measurement of success. There are brands who prefer to stay below the radar and focus their time, energy, and resources on making their world a better place. Or some companies don't have the budgets to orchestrate sustained PR programs that reach millions of people. Businesses like Taylor Guitars, H. G. Fenton, Academy for Professional Excellence, Leaders Quest, TRU Colors Brewing, Mama Chia, Sunrun (solar service), Gildan (apparel), and Biggby Coffee are beautifully run companies that you may have never heard of.

Other companies:

https://consciouscompanymedia.com/sustainable-business/the-worlds-top-25-for-benefit-companies/

Dr. Bronners (Vista, CA)
TerraCycle (Trenton, NJ)
Impact Makers (Richmond, VA)
New Resource Bank (San Francisco, CA)
Method (San Francisco, CA)
NovoNordisk (Aktieselskab, Denmark)
MicroEnsure (UK)
Recology (San Francisco, CA)
EILEEN FISHER (Irvington, NY)
Natura (Brazil)
Etsy
Aveda
TOMS
ME to WE

Every business has the opportunity to be remarkable. Size doesn't matter. Location doesn't matter. Industry doesn't matter. Purpose matters. Character matters. Leaders have the choice to do business anyway they see fit. A beautiful business works in an ever-evolving fashion. It's more likely that it will shape a one-hundred-year vision than a business that's built on a quick-exit strategy. It's an entity that's led by people who are willing to do the deep and hard work to take a stand for something they wholeheartedly believe in and put products and services in front of their customers that make a difference to them. Making this choice to build and run a purposeful business creates its own magnetism. It attracts those with similar values into their orbit. It won't be done at a hackathon or through a research thinktank. It's unlikely to be shaped by the linear business-building processes taught in many MBA programs. It may go against *big data*. It will be done by deeply caring and hardworking leaders who are driven by something much more than profit alone, cash-outs, or the VC-backed longshot.

Why Evolve?

❝ People only change their ways when what they truly value is threatened.

— MARSHALL GOLDSMITH, *WHAT GOT YOU HERE WON'T GET YOU THERE: HOW SUCCESSFUL PEOPLE BECOME EVEN MORE SUCCESSFUL*

Your organization may be at the point where it's humming along nicely. You've got your fair share of customers; your business is making money and your customers are delighted. You're also facing your fair share of challenges and obstacles.

If you're like many businesses large and small, you're looking out at the horizon as far as you can see. And you're looking to see the unseeable, your future. You're thinking about where your business is going, how you're doing against the competition and how it's meeting the needs of customers. You know, on some level, there's room for improvement and you want to have more control over your destiny and shape the future of your business.

If you're in the "my business is thriving" category, congratulations! However, if you're like most businesses, at some point you'll find yourself closer to the "my business is struggling" category. You may be there today, or it may happen next week, month, or year.

So why bother evolving your brand and business into one that makes a big impact on the world? After all, isn't business primarily about making money?

Consider this.

Each of us, whether we're business leaders or not, has a finite amount of time on this lovely planet. We're blessed with the precious gift of life. It's a privilege to be alive. If you're anything like me, you've hit the lottery—to be born in a place and time with so much possibility, so much abundance, so much opportunity, so much information, and so many resources at your fingertips . . . and it would be a shame to squander such gifts. We're born into a human body with the ability to move worlds. We're blessed with the gifts of thought, strategy, creativity, and imagination.

As a business owner or leader, you've either earned or have been given power. That power allows you to make decisions that affect people's lives, people's livelihoods, your culture, your customers, your community, and, yes, the planet. How you make those decisions, what you base those decisions on, and why you make those decisions has exponential effects.

Why go to the trouble and expense of a brand evolution? The answer is simple and compelling. All businesses need to evolve in order to thrive. Your business landscape is always changing, your customers are moving, your market is shifting, your competitors are adapting, and you can't afford to be left behind.

New competitors arrive on the scene seemingly daily. Customers interests, tastes, and habits are changing. Technology does its own form of disruption, and a wide variety of factors shift the dynamics of the marketplace. As Darwin pointed out, the species that fails to adapt and evolve goes extinct.

Businesses Build on Purpose

> **❝ The Zen master would say if you want to change government, you have to aim at changing corporations, and if you want to change corporations, you first have to change the consumers. Whoa, wait a minute! The consumer? That's me. You mean I'm the one who has to change?**

— YVON CHOUINARD, *LET MY PEOPLE GO SURFING*

My experience has taught me that the most self-aware
and thoughtful of business leaders are on a mission to
make a difference in the world, whether or not they're
consciously aware of it. They've been around the block
enough times to realize that when people pull together
in a common purpose, exponential results come. Many
of them care about far more than simply the financial
gains of the company, and they care about profit, too.
They care deeply about how they go about creating their
financial gain. Some of the most successful of them use
a wide array of measuring sticks that include, but are not
limited to, customer satisfaction (net promoter scores),
product or service quality, employee engagement and
satisfaction, happiness ratios, work-life integration,
cultural engagement and turnover, supply-chain
efficiencies, community service and impact metrics,
support of causes and give-back programs, customer
satisfaction and loyalty, social and environmental impact
metrics, market and industry respect, and financial
health including profit and growth.

There are clear trends of multimeasured success
beyond profit in industries that include consumer
products, consumer electronics, software, technology,
retail, travel and hospitality, education, sports and
entertainment, professional services, financial services,
health care, and biotech. In common, the best of the best
work and live for more. It is as if some larger guiding force
drives these business leaders.

For those companies that are interested in pursuing
a formalized path for metrics beyond profit, there are a
couple of options in both certification and legal structure.
The term "B Corp," as certified by B Lab, is often used
interchangeably to refer to benefit corporations
(sometimes called public benefit corporations) and
Certified B Corporations. However, these are actually
distinctly different entities with a connected history.

A benefit corporation is a legal business entity for companies who have applied for and passed a certification, similar to Fair Trade or USDA Organic certification. Further, B Lab, the nonprofit organization that runs the B Corporation certification process, was also involved in the benefit corporation legislation, which now requires Certified B Corporations to become benefit corporations if that legal entity structure is available in the state that the business is incorporated in. So, while a "B Corp" and a "benefit corporation" may be similar in concept, there are critical differences.

The B Corp

B Corp is the term used for a for-profit business entity that has been certified by the nonprofit B Lab as choosing to meet higher standards of transparency, accountability, and performance. Any for-profit entity can be a B Corp provided it is certified by B Lab, meets their stated requirement, and keeps up with applicable membership fees. The B Lab assessment analyzes many things about the business's operations with over two hundred questions that cover, for example, the quality standards of its products and services, how the business treats its workers and the environment, and the extent to which the business supports its community. The foundational thinking behind being a B Corp is to do well by doing good but also to be transparent and accountable in measuring what matters and reporting on it.

Again, you might think of it as the Certified USDA Organic certification for businesses intentionally working to do well by doing good.

The Benefit Corporation

In contrast, the benefit corporation is a legal corporate structure or type of corporation. The reason many get confused about the differences between a B Corp and benefit corporation is that the latter emerged from the B Corp movement. This structure was created because some entrepreneurs believed that the B Corp certification could not offer the form of legal protection that a government-recognized legal structure could provide.

So unlike a B Corp, which can be any type of for-profit legal entity, such as an LLC, Corp, or S Corp, a benefit corporation is a type of corporation. Should you be interested in more information for either a B Corp or benefit corporation, visit the following links:

B Corp: https://bcorporation.net/

Benefit corporation: https://benefitcorp.net/

Conscious Capitalism

Based on the best-selling book by Raj Sisodia and John Mackey, Conscious Capitalism is a wide and active nonprofit organization. With satellite chapters across the US, at universities, and globally, Conscious Capitalism works to support a global community of business leaders dedicated to elevating humanity through business. With the aim to demonstrate that capitalism is a powerful force for good when practiced consciously, the organization provides learning exchanges, conferences, training, and transformational storytelling. This organization is a collective of like-minded businesspeople who bond together over its belief-based tenets.

From their credo: "Conscious Capitalism is a way of thinking about capitalism and business that better reflects where we are in the human journey, the state of our world today, and the innate potential of business to make a positive impact on the world. Conscious businesses are galvanized by higher purposes that serve, align, and integrate the interests of all their major stakeholders."[41]

It's worth noting that Conscious Capitalism Press is the publisher of this book, and I have been an active participant in this community.

Regardless if you decide to pursue either of the above paths to formalize your stance in either certification or business structure, deciding to take a stand for what you believe is the first step.

The heart of this guiding force for business is the answer to the question posed previously—your *why* or your purpose. The question and the actionable answer to it may be the single most important thing you do for your business, for your people, for your brand, and for the world around you. It is the question that constantly sits at the heart of your company and one that you constantly ask, answer, and perpetuate into action as you continue. To answer it is to both stand for something and do something about what you stand for. To answer it clearly is to know the soul of your company and the heart of your brand. To put it into action and consistently hold your company accountable for it is walking your talk. For your company to live the answer to your purpose is to work with self-awareness.

Just like the humans who create and grow a business entity, companies and brands are living, conscious, creative, evolving, adapting, and growing entities that need constant care and attention. And they need a reason for being in order to thrive. Business leaders and the employees of a business should have a clear understanding of why they're doing what they're doing.

Why Should Anyone Care about *Why*?

There's a well-known quote by Simon Sinek that states, "People don't buy WHAT you do, they buy WHY you do it." While Simon has done and continues to do an exceptional job popularizing and evangelizing the ideas within his book *Start With Why*, he's not the first. Its history can be traced back as far as Aristotle, and he can likely be credited with this notion. In her best-selling book *Grit*,[42] Angela Duckworth points out that Aristotle was among the first to recognize that there are at least two ways to pursue happiness. He called one "eudemonic"—in harmony with one's good (*eu*) inner spirit (*daemon*). And the other is "hedonic," which is aimed at positive, pleasure-in-the-moment, inherently self-centered experiences. The term hedonism is derived from this.

Aristotle took a clear side on the issue, believing the hedonic approach to life is crude and primitive, and perpetuated the eudemonic life as an honorable and pure pursuit. Both of these approaches to the pursuit of happiness have very deep evolutionary roots. Humans seek pleasure because, by and large, the things that bring us pleasure are those that increase our chances of survival. Our descendants' craving for food and sex helped to ensure they lived longer and reproduced.

Conversely, we humans have evolved to seek meaning and purpose. Elemental to our way of being, we seek belonging, leading to the drive to connect with and serve others prompting survival. Individuals and groups who cooperate are more likely to survive than loners. Nature demonstrates that individuals who are creative, giving, diverse, and cooperative are much more likely to survive and thrive. Lions hunt in prides, apes flourish in a troop, baboons live in a congress, geese migrate in flocks, coyotes thrive in bands, wolves live in packs, and so on. A healthy living experience depends on stable interpersonal relationships and community that feeds us in many ways, shelters us from the elements, and protects us from harms. Our desire to connect is as basic a human need as our appetite for pleasure.

There's a well-known story about John F. Kennedy that unfolds during a visit to the NASA space center in 1962. President Kennedy noticed a janitor carrying a broom. He interrupted his tour, walked over to the man, and said, "Hi, I'm Jack Kennedy. What do you do here?"

"Well, Mr. President," the janitor responded, "I'm helping put a man on the moon."

That janitor knew his work of keeping the building clean was tethered to a larger purpose. And when your business understands and embraces that belief system and puts it into action, astonishing things happen.

In the end, an evolved brand creates organizational integrity that leads to a beautiful business. Integrity is the interconnected state of being whole, where the separate parts of the organization operate congruently with one another. What a company believes, how it operates, and how it's seen by the world are brought together in integrity.

Along with your people, your brand is your business's greatest asset. If properly understood and integrated to work in harmony, your brand and people can create the difference between a great business and an average one that struggles to survive. Built and leveraged properly, your evolved brand holds the key to accelerating growth and profitability, building customer loyalty, attracting and retaining employees, and creating long-term value. Yet the word "brand" can create both confusion and misconception, and hiring an expert brand partner is too often misjudged and mismanaged.

Understanding Your Brand

Before we go too much further, let me remind you of some of the foundations that are important for the context between business and brand. I covered this in the first chapter of this book, but for the sake of clarity, I'll reinforce these ideas here.

A beautiful business is a journey, a way of doing business, instigated by the leader's or leadership teams' awakening to an evolved brand. In order to evolve toward a beautiful business, you need to understand both the relationship between a business and a brand. It's my belief that the two are inseparable.

In metaphorical terms, a complete human being is parallel to a business. Let's say that you, the reader, who is a person, is the business. Your physiological systems within your biology, such as your pulmonary system, digestive system, immune system, and sensory systems, make up the systems within your business. If they shut down, you as a business are threatened. But these biological systems don't come close to defining all of you. Add to this, all of your beliefs, psychology, character, persona, and behaviors that are driven by these characteristics, along with how you express yourself, and that is your brand and culture. This includes what you say and do, the manner in which you communicate, the clothes you choose to wear, the environment you choose to live in, the car you drive, the people you associate with, the tribes you belong to, and all of your stylistic and expressionistic elements. In the psychological world, this would be characterized as your persona or personality. The brand is the intentional fusion of all character-defining attributes that come from what you believe and how you see and express yourself. Again, your brand is your character. The impact this creates on others is your brand reputation.

Further Defining the Brand

Your brand is a montage of concepts, beliefs, strategies, language, and visual elements that are synthesized together and expressed consistently to create a unified effect. The ingredients that make up your brand include your core organizational beliefs, including your purpose, promise, and values. They also include your persona or archetype, which is the character stance you take in your business. Your persona can also help define your market position. More on this later.

Your brand also includes all the language and the tone and voice of that language that you use to communicate what you believe, do, and offer. It includes your marketing messaging, positioning statements, tagline, and all the design elements that visually represent your brand. Your brand also includes your culture, which is how you operate, communicate, and behave. These varied elements should all be carefully and thoughtfully developed and orchestrated to consistently communicate and harmonize your unique position.

Over time and applied consistently, the culmination of all the attributes creates your brand reputation—what people say about and, more importantly, how they feel about your company. This brand reputation, also referred to as perception or impact, is the culmination of how anyone experiences your organization. Your brand reputation is how they see you, how they understand you, how they feel about you, and how they talk about you.

If a brand is something people experience, then it must convey a wide range of sensory information. You see it, hear it, touch it, say it, and feel it. Your brand must be both understood and felt, and therefore it must contain intellectual elements that are clear and emotional elements that are moving. It must be unique to you, which creates your market differentiation.

A successful brand is as much an idea, notion, or feeling that's held in the hearts and minds of your audiences as a tangible thing they can see and touch. This idea or feeling is what your customers come to trust that you will consistently deliver on, because you've done it so consistently over time. That's important, because great and beautiful ideas are the secret sauce of prosperous companies.

Your brand, therefore, is not your logo, your signage, your storefront, your website, or your tagline—although each are elements to your brand. Without unifying beliefs and an underlying strategy that orchestrates all of your brand's touchpoints, you'll never have a trusted brand that creates consistent impact, loyalty, and long-term value.

Kit of Parts That Makes the Whole

There is a congregation of brand touchpoints that builds people's perception of your company. Every time you do any marketing, communication, advertising, public relations, presentation, or promotion, you are presenting your brand and forging people's perception of it.

So how do you go about composing your efforts around something so comprehensive and dispersed?

As noted above, a brand reputation is not what you say it is; it's what they say it is. It's what people might say about your company when you're not in the room to explain it or defend it.

The foundational truth about an evolved brand is that it's all about creating one essential human thing: trust. The reputation your company has is the position it will hold in the hearts and minds of your audiences. Your reputation is, perhaps, your most valuable asset. If people trust you, they do business with you.

In Trust, We Trust

> **❝ It takes twenty years to build a reputation and five minutes to ruin it.**
>
> —WARREN BUFFETT

> **❝ The glue that holds all relationships together—including the relationship between the leader and the led—is trust, and trust is based on integrity.**
>
> —BRIAN TRACY

As noted previously, trust and reliability are not the same thing. Someone who consistently treats you poorly is showing reliable behavior but shouldn't be trusted. Trust makes you feel good and is valuable in all good relationships. Small, consistent, and meaningful actions, over time, build and maintain trust. People trust what they understand and what constantly delivers value to them.

In the world of branding, slick exterior or brand presentation may not be a trusted company. When you have integrity between what you say and what you do, trust builds. Trust comes from our way of being in the world that is consistent with what and how we communicate.

Brands looking to build lasting relationships with their customers (a.k.a. brand loyalty) need to first build trust. Few people get confused into buying something they don't understand, but customers also don't buy products they aren't emotionally engaged with and that they don't trust.

There's a subtle, yet important, distinction between **trust** and **belief**.

Trust is a general feeling based on one's perception of the source. For someone to trust your brand, they must feel good about it. This usually is a transfer or extension on behalf of the one trusting, hence the term "extending your trust." Trusting can be risky. By trusting a brand, the customer is hoping the brand will deliver on its promise.

Belief, on the other hand, tends to be something that is grounded in either facts or experiences. For instance, if a customer has a string of exceptional experiences with your brand or product, they will not only *trust* your brand, but they will *believe* that you will continue to deliver. Belief also is often an alignment in values. If you know what a brand believes in and they live up to those beliefs, you'll have confidence in that brand, which is more firmly rooted than *trust*.

Trust is like blood pressure. It's silent, vital to good health, and if abused it can be deadly.

—FRANK SONNENBERG

Said simply: trust is offered; belief is earned.

During one stage of the brand evolution process, I spend focused time in defining anchored "reasons to believe" (RTBs), which are proof points that support the brand promise. Without these RTBs, customers need to extend their trust. With them, they begin their belief journey.

Think of it this way. Picture a brand you believe in or one you don't. Now, ask yourself, "Because of the brand's actions, am I willing to extend trust to them?" Answer yes or no. Is that because of what they did or how you feel about what they did? Chances are it's both, and especially how their actions made you feel.

For me, that was Audi. Once I believed, but now I don't trust. Even though I owned a vehicle that was not affected by their emission scandals, I have significantly diminished belief in their brand, and even in what they say about their company. And, thanks to their well-documented dishonest deeds, I have ceased extending trust to them. Audi will now have to work to rebuild trust with its customers. That will likely take years, and they won't win every customer back.

The Necessity of Trust in a Culture

Patrick Lencioni is the author of *The Five Dysfunctions of a Team*. In this leadership parable book, Patrick reveals the basics of teamwork by using a story of a technology company that is facing challenges in growth and customer acquisition. As the parable unfolds, the fictional new CEO, Catherine Petersen, sees potential in the organization and its people. However, the leadership team is not aligned or unified. This creates a negative cascading effect on the entire team. As the story unfolds, the author identifies trust as a linchpin issue, which in turn affects the team's ability to thrive. The inhibitors, according to the book, are the absence of trust, fear of conflict, lack of commitment, avoidance of accountability, and inattention to results.

I've seen this story unfold in real life. Much of the work I do with corporate cultures is designed to investigate the level of trust on the team and that team's unifying beliefs that create trust: purpose, values, vision, and promise. Without trust in a culture, teams don't have the ability to engage in healthy debate, they will avoid conflict, accountability, commitment, and focus on results. The antidote for this is to create this unifying belief-based framework—again, purpose, values, vision, and promise— and to ensure an environment to live in. I promise you this, if you don't have trust in your team, you don't have a unified team. And because of this, you will fall short of many of your goals, or you'll burn out the team in driving to create them.

What's at Stake?

When applying this to brands who want loyal and lasting relationships, a company needs to be clear about their brand promise and go to great lengths to live up to it.

Your brand promise and the effects that come from delivering on it create the foundation for a lasting and loyal audience. So if you want brand loyalty, you have to act consistently from your values so that customers believe your promise.

Think of Starbucks

There are more than fourteen thousand Starbucks across the globe. Part of the reason there can be so many Starbucks is that in every store you enter and order from, you can get your preferred drink made the same way, for the same relative cost, in the same relative time. It's human nature for people to trust what they understand, what they feel good about, and what's consistent.

What shows up consistently we trust. When we can get our favorite Starbucks drink served consistently in the Seattle airport, in Miami, in Milan, and in our own neighborhood, we trust it to be consistent and reliable. The trust that comes from consistency and reliability is part of the reason many chain stores like MacDonald's, Jamba, Target, Trader Joe's, and many others thrive.

There are both tangibles and intangibles that contribute to the perception of your company. The reason that Harley-Davidson riders will pay as much as 20 percent more for similar motorcycles than Honda, for instance, is the intangible value that comes with belonging to the Harley-Davidson tribe. At the time of writing this book, a large latte at Dunkin (donuts) costs around $2.49, whereas a venti (20 oz.) latte at Starbucks costs $4.15. The manner in which your brand is expressed sets the stage for expectations (a.k.a. brand promises) for your company to deliver on, which when delivered consistently increases the trust, loyalty, and value of your brand. Your brand identity, colors, typography, and imagery are just some of the visual components, but contrary to some misconceptions, this is not the core of your brand. These visual elements combined with your beliefs, messaging, and ultimately your brand story can evoke a range of powerful emotions, perceptions, and understandings that set up the opportunity for a trusting relationship between your company and its customers.

Your brand story—the fusion of your visual and verbal brand components told and shared in a story format—can support or detract from your company's credibility and work to differentiate your company from competitors. Ultimately, the way your organization expresses itself carves out your position in the market. How your company communicates its values, beliefs, products, services, and stories can be significantly different than your competitors. This defines your brand position.

How to earn belief:

1. **Know your brand promise and make sure your brand can live up to it.** For example, Subway promises to "deliver healthy food fast." They seem to live up to that.
2. **Build your RTBs.** Create and articulate clear RTBs to support your promise. These should be simple but factual. Once people begin to trust your promise, they'll want to know more. RTBs back up what you promise to deliver. RTBs help to transition your brand into a believable one.
3. **Live the promise.** The actions of your brand should live in accordance with the promises you state. People believe in consistent action—the more consistent, the better. This is why the franchise model works so well. People support predictability, and they want their expectations to be met.
4. **Repeat and deliver.** Over time you must live up to your promise. All media touchpoints must have a clear intent and manner in which they reinforce the promise. Some will echo the promise, and some will deliver RTBs. LinkedIn, for instance, is an ideal platform to reinforce the RTBs due to the robust media you can serve up there, and it's a more personal channel, so more customer intimacy can be created.

66 The people when rightly and fully trusted will return the trust.

— ABRAHAM LINCOLN

Outcomes That Matter

Beautiful Business Goals: Aiming for the Right Outcomes

At the onset of this book, I asked a question that people have indirectly asked me when considering an evolution into a beautiful business: **"Why should anyone care about beauty when business is about results?"**

In truth, this question really could be broken down into four definable areas. Who is "anyone"? What do you "care" about? What is "beauty"? And what kind of "results" are we talking about? In chapter 2, I discussed the meaning and value of beauty and therefore the beautiful business. In chapter 4, I talked about *who* might *care* about a beautiful business, and what *they* might care about. And, in this chapter I'll overview, but stop short of instructing, what types of *result* measurements you might consider. Going further, in this chapter, I'll provide a guiding overview of some of the things to think about measuring for success, and I've created a free workbook designed to guide you to a set of implementable outcomes. **You can download your free workbook at www.the-beautiful-business.com.**

—

The reason I'm stopping short of instructing you on what to measure is that business leaders must, in their own way, define what to measure based on their unique business value system. One of my favorite questions when getting immersed in the world of my clients is "What does success look like for you and your team?" How a leader answers this begins to reveal what matters most to them and thus creates some indication of where their underlying value system sits, including alluding to their true purpose for being in business.

What you choose to measure is a reflection of what you value. The results of these choices will vary from business to business. Because I cannot tell you what to value, or what your belief matrix—your purpose, vision, values, and promise—should be, I cannot tell you what you should measure. Instead, I'm going to provide some approaches to help you choose among a menu of options to consider measuring in four key quadrants: resources, leadership, culture, and customers.

Within each of these areas, I'll offer some perspective and options of attributes to consider measuring. I encourage you to see this process and the choices of measurements behind them as a starting point—but by no means an exhaustive list—of what you should consider measuring. You will find or discover, in your own way, what to measure. The measurement options I'll offer come from a variety of resources. Some will be more scientific- or metric-oriented than others. Some you may have heard of, such as Net Promoter Score. Some might feel somewhat esoteric, such as organizational consciousness. Some things that you might measure will be tangible, such as customer loyalty. Some will be far less tangible, such as individual fulfillment. With this, I'll dispel a myth in the business world. Just because something is more difficult to measure with tangible outcomes doesn't make those attributes any less valuable.

Here's an example. Some time ago I was working with a global organization that was experiencing conflicts within their culture. When the organization's leaders came to me, they felt strongly, at first, that the issue was around lack of core values on their team. This was—and is—an extremely high-performing team that had just over three hundred employees working in seven different countries. While their primary headquarters were in the USA, their functional teams were spread across various time zones and many worked remotely. Communication challenges added complexity to team dynamics. After being hired, one of my first steps was to design and employ a culture benchmarking study that included a company-wide survey, several focus groups, and one-on-one conversations with individuals from all levels and functional teams. After implementing the survey and analyzing the data, the benchmarking revealed several issues, but primarily the team had trust issues, with one another and with leadership. It may seem odd, but it's not uncommon for high-performing teams to have low levels of trust. These trust issues came from a low level of team and individual self-awareness. As a group, we set out on a year-long process to improve team trust and self-awareness and to construct additional ways to measure organizational success.

Here's the point. Neither trust nor self-awareness are particularly easy or obvious to benchmark, and they may even feel like abstract or touchy-feely soft skills. However, to this team, they created significant limitations, even though they were already high performers. The good news for this team was that by unearthing the unconscious issues, they transformed the obstacles and turned them into opportunities. While this team was performing at a high level, the work done to instill deeper trust and self-awareness in their culture created even greater results for both their top and bottom lines but also improved team engagement, collaboration, innovation, and communication while lowering turnover.

Part of the result was to incorporate an ongoing culture measurement set that measured team trust and team and individual self-awareness, among other values, into their HR and employee recruitment and review systems. We also designed a series of self-awareness questions in their employee prospecting and interviewing processes, which helped to measure the amount of self-awareness in potential candidates. For this business, the right questions led to more of the right outcomes.

Measuring outcomes often begins with getting to the right questions. In my consulting work, I have some "go-to" questions I ask to help assess how or if I can effectively serve the company and, if so, how they might look at success. In the context of this book and the chapter here, I offer these questions to help you begin to discern what is most important to you to consider measuring. I invite you to sit with these questions and answer the ones that call to you most. Once you've done this, look for gaps in your current business environment to help determine what you may want to work toward measuring and improving upon. I share these questions because they can be a start to determining what you might want to measure at your company:

- What do you want (tangible and intangible) that you don't have now?
- What does success look like? And what is the biggest obstacle in the way of that success?
- How do you define and measure performance?
- What does a healthy business look like for you? What does a healthy culture look like?
- What is your role (as a leader)?
- What is the most critical decision you're facing right now?
- If you had a magic wand and the power to change a few key things in your business, what would you change and why?

- If your wise future self could give you advice or a question to ask, what would it be?
- What are you most [certain, uncertain, pleased, unhappy, etc.] about?
- In what ways are you and your team complicit in the unwanted outcomes you're currently experiencing?

There is no right or wrong recipe, no measurement commandments, no fixed or perfect measurement mix that I can offer you without knowing what your beliefs and values are. I can only offer possible considerations on which to measure what success might look like for your company. To do otherwise is to offer questions that are unhelpful and that may not truly fit your business. My invitation to you, within this chapter, is to look through the variety of options I present here and others that you may have in your tool kit, and then come to your own unique recipe of success-defining outcomes on which to focus.

So then, what kinds of results is the beautiful business leader looking for?

As you start to get glimmerings of which outcomes might matter to you and your company, you start thinking about how to make them manifest. Before you take that step, I'm going to talk about a framework for the journey to achieve your outcomes.

Orienting the Strategy: The Journey to the Outcomes You Want

In its simplest terms a strategy says, "We're going here. We're creating this. Here's why. And we'll do it in this timeframe."

Here's how I see the difference between vision, goals, and strategies.

A **goal** is an outcome you want.

A **strategy** is a plan to realize that outcome.

A **vision** is how the world begins to look as you realize your purpose-oriented goals.

Most important is that all your activities (goals, strategy, and vision) ultimately work to serve and achieve your **purpose**.

A **goal** without a **strategy** is a dream.

A **strategy** without a **vision** is a to-do list.

A **vision** without a **purpose** lacks a meaningful reason for being.

Creating a clear and motivating strategy starts with your purpose and vision. Your business vision is like a movie trailer—a succinct and descriptive narrative—of what you envision your business becoming based on your purpose. When you tell this vision through the lens of a story, you and your team can more clearly see what the future state of your business can be as you go about achieving your purpose. As you use this movie trailer metaphor, you can more clearly articulate the promised land your business is headed toward.

Business goals should be clearly stated: how your company will attract and retain the right customers and employees; how the people inside your organization will be affected by the work; how you'll succeed in the marketplace; how you'll manage and maximize the necessary resources; how you'll create products and/or services; and what success looks like for your company.

Business goals are the lifeblood of the organization, and a clear strategy provides direction and vision. A good strategy is like a blueprint or map that's easy to understand, clear enough to follow, and motivating for the team. As the late, great New York Yankee philosopher Yogi Berra said, "You got to be very careful if you don't know where you're going, because you might not get there."

Gardening as Metaphor for Outcomes

Think of a garden. The intent behind your garden is your purpose. Let's say that this, for the gardeners of the New York City High Line, is to create transformational experiences that bring people from the city closer to nature and the beauty it offers. The driving actions of the gardeners—planning, planting, and tending the garden—are defined by their values. In the gardener's world, this might mean using native plants, it might mean valuing fertilizers that come naturally from local sources, and it might mean recapturing treated grey water in a sustainable manner. When the gardener is planning "what's next" (the strategy) in the garden, they're looking ahead and asking, "What can we do next to achieve our purpose?" Then the gardener plans and creates milestones and puts their gardening into action. From there, the gardener can define a set of metrics for success in the High Line.

However, the garden is never really done. There will always be more garden visitors to inspire and to connect with nature, and each season and year brings different situations that change the garden. And one day, the lead gardener will retire. Then it's up to the next leadership generation of gardeners to pick up the shovel, plan what's next, and move forward. Is success a good harvest? The number of visitors? Beautiful flowers? Is it a garden future generations can enjoy? Measurement outcomes will look different for different types of gardens. The actions that lead to measurement in all varying gardens is an ongoing journey. *Measuring* is an active verb—something that continues and that needs the frequent touchstone of the purpose and vision. This year's annuals die in the fall. What do we plant next year that meets the vision we have for the garden?

To answer the driving and orienting questions above, there are three primary concerns for the gardener: *right reasons, right strategy, right actions*. Right reasons come from your purpose and vision. Right strategy builds on the right reasons and defines your direction. Right actions are the tactical doings that generate the outcomes that loop back to your right reasons.

What Gets Measured Gets Done

Think again of your garden. Your garden is your business. In earlier chapters we've primed the soil and planted the seeds for the foundation of your business by cultivating your purpose, vision, values, and promise. Now that your garden is planted, it's time to start thinking about what you'll want to harvest. It's time to think about the longevity of the health of your garden. And it's time to start thinking about how your garden is both affected by and influences the things that go beyond your garden walls.

Any healthy garden, just like a beautiful business, relies on a symbiotic working relationship with resources. In order to flourish, your business relies on the unified efforts of the people within your business. The people within your business rely on all the resources that enable the individuals and team to flourish. These symbiotic resources include all the people that contribute to your business, especially its leaders, the customers your business serves through your products and services, the time financial resources that are required to keep your business thriving, the communities in which your business has relationships, and the natural and environmental resources that are required to run your business, to name a few. A garden or business that doesn't give attention to these symbiotic relationships is thinking short term.

If your business has the vision, for instance, to be around one hundred years from now, or even next year, you have to consider the relationships, responsibilities, and replenishability of the resources required to flourish.

If your business is garden-like, then you, as a gardener, must also be thinking about the health, care, growth, and sustainability of your garden business. If your garden is expecting to harvest some of the growth that each season brings, you'll be careful to give close attention to what's required for a healthy, sustainable, flourishing entity. As such, the business gardener should be thinking about what to count, qualify, and measure in order to sustain and grow.

In the world of the beautiful business, there is an expansive set of realms to consider when developing meaningful metrics. A beautiful business includes, but goes beyond, the usual measuring sticks that include net revenue, profit, employee turnover, cost to acquire a customer, net promoter scores (NPS), etc. As the leader of a beautiful business, you can and should come up with your own system of what to measure, because how you define success in your business might be very different than what a *competitor* in the same market might consider successful.

Evolved leaders create, curate, and fixate on defining and measuring their own set of metrics and KPIs that inspire their self-defined success. Their self-defined KPIs are their strategy. Both they and their people know it. By creating their own set of metrics, they can lead the business through their ultimate journey, not just manage it. This is not a subtle distinction.

One former Amazon executive recounts, "At Amazon, everything that can be measured is. Every piece of data is tested and analyzed—not just web design or product features, but finance, HR, and operations processes. . . . More than anyone I've ever met, Bezos knew that things don't improve unless they're measured."[43] Having worked with Amazon I can attest to their relentless pursuit of measuring everything they can, and focusing on their own set of self-defined metrics to determining success. The company's founder, Jeff Bezos, oversees what he calls Amazon's "culture of metrics."[44]

I take the risk of citing Amazon as an example for how you can measure nearly everything within business operations. I do not believe that Amazon demonstrates that they are beautiful business. To my knowledge, Amazon does not measure a wide range of things that many beautiful businesses would measure, including but not limited to employee satisfaction, diversity, equity, or inclusion, or social or environmental responsibilities.

While what you decide to measure should be driven by what you value as an organization, there are a couple of models worth considering when looking at measurement outcomes. With this, I'll share a high-level overview of the measurement systems created by B Lab and Conscious Capitalism.

The Foundations for an Evolved Set of Success Metrics

In 1987, Josh Mailman and Wayne Silby created a nonprofit membership organization of socially responsible business leaders who were working toward and committed to creating a more just and sustainable world. This was the founding of Social Venture Network, now called Social Venture Circle. The foundation of this pioneering organization laid the runway for the creation of subsequent organizations such as Conscious Capitalism (a term and organization coined and popularized by John Mackey, Whole Foods cofounder, and Raj Sisodia, professor of marketing at Bentley University, in their book *Conscious Capitalism*); B Lab (the nonprofit that certifies B Corporations); and Great Place to Work. These are among some of the earliest pioneers of what's now called the conscious business movement. Each deserves credit for their unique roles in serving business leaders with a new horizon of potential that fosters a more conscious approach for capitalism to serve and elevate humanity.

What "Conscious Capitalists" Measure

In January of 2013, *Harvard Business Review* published a book that helped to ignite a business groundswell directed at demonstrating and designing business as a force for good: *Conscious Capitalism: Liberating the Heroic Spirit of Business*. History has taught us that free-enterprise capitalism is among the most powerful systems for cultural cooperation and human progress ever conceived.

The book's central thesis was that the potential for business to elevate ever more people out of poverty and create sustainable prosperity around the world was an attainable vision—if only we could aspire to an evolved consciousness about the interconnectedness of all stakeholders and resources impacted by our businesses.

This evolved business mindset centered on a wider set of metrics in which the business gives it attention to, aims for, and measures. There are four fundamental principles to Conscious Capitalism: Higher Purpose, Conscious Culture, Stakeholder Integration, and Conscious Leadership. As I've discussed throughout this book, the purpose of an organization has to be higher than just making money. Stakeholders, not just shareholders, in a Conscious Capitalist business must understand that a healthy business is a sustainable ecosystem, which will not thrive without all aspects of the system being in harmony and integrity. This means all the stakeholders, including the employees and the customers, must be in alignment with the purpose. Leadership in a Conscious Capitalist business centers their role on defining the purpose, setting the vision, establishing the values, creating integrity for the needs of the business and the stakeholders, and inspiring aligned actions. Business culture consists of the values, principles, and rituals of the business and how these attributes show up as consistent and aligned behaviors.

At its essence, consciousness simply means being more conscious of more attributes. This begins with organizational self-awareness—the willingness to look inside and around, acknowledge shortcomings, limitations, uncertainties, and fears, and take responsibility for our actions and how these actions affect the inside and outside of the company. While profits aren't overlooked in Conscious Capitalism, the focused behaviors that drive profit are done so with an integrated ecosystem that aligns the interests of all company stakeholders.

The Four Tenets of Conscious Capitalism

Higher Purpose

When organizations cultivate and work with purpose, they offer stakeholders a clear and actionable *why*. Here are some examples of purpose (sometimes referred to as mission) statements that represent a higher purpose:

- **Patagonia:** Build the best product, cause no unnecessary harm, use business to inspire, and implement solutions to the environmental crisis.
- **LinkedIn:** To connect the world's professionals to make them more productive and successful.
- **Asana:** To help humanity thrive by enabling all teams to work together effortlessly.
- **Warby Parker:** To offer designer eyewear at a revolutionary price while leading the way for socially conscious businesses.
- **Intuit:** To improve its customers' financial lives so profoundly, they couldn't imagine going back to the old way.
- **JetBlue:** To inspire humanity—both in the air and on the ground.

When an organization identifies and articulates a clear and actionable purpose, as these examples show, it empowers them to activate and align around a singular metric on which to strive for. When an organization creates a purpose, they have a single, unifying metric: the purpose metric. This metric is both a rallying cry for all stakeholders and the ultimate metric that you're striving for. When creating a purpose metric, you'll want to:

1. Ensure that all stakeholders in your organization have access to it and understand its importance

2. Ensure that your stakeholders can see how you are on the road to fulfill your purpose
3. Enable each person to understand how their role directly impacts the purpose

This is one of the most vital and powerful things in uniting the team around a purpose-cause and igniting them together aligned in the purpose.

In measuring your purpose, it is also essential that you understand the stakeholder impact. Is your purpose effectively inspiring employees? Are customers choosing your products above others in part because of your purpose? Are your partners, suppliers, and investors aligned with your purpose?

Conscious Leadership

An organizational culture will mimic the character of the actions and personality of the individual at the top. As above, so below. The more self-aware or conscious the leadership team is of their beliefs and the impacts of their actions on the company, the more conscious they are. Conscious leaders inspire loyalty, elevate the character of the team, and consistently set standards for high performance in their teams.

Conscious Culture

Culture can be defined as the culmination of the values and principles that constitute the social and moral fabric of a business. Culture shows up in action and stories. A conscious culture is one where the principles of Conscious Capitalism permeate the organization and inspire a spirit of trust and cooperation among all stakeholders. A values-based culture is one that is intentional about how people act and perform. When a culture is not defined, encouraged, and enforced, the people in the organization aren't all moving in the same direction.

Organizational Consciousness

Barrett Values Centre / FULL SPECTRUM CONSCIOUSNESS®

Based on the work of Richard Barrett, the Barrett Values Centre evolutionary model of development of personal and organizational values is built on the work of Abraham Maslow's Hierarchy of Needs. This work has been vetted and tested over more than two decades of real-world experience with thousands of organizations. The model identifies the seven key areas that encompass human motivations. These motivations range from basic survival on one end to service and concern for future generations at the other.

Why Are Full Spectrum Organizations Successful?

Full Spectrum Organizations, according to Barrett, pay attention to everything that is important, and they display all the positive attributes of the Seven Levels of Organizational Consciousness. Within the model, organizations master:

- Survival Consciousness by focusing on *profit, financial stability*, and the *health and safety of employees*
- Relationship Consciousness by focusing on *open communication, employee recognition*, and *customer satisfaction*
- Self-esteem Consciousness by focusing on *performance, results, quality, excellence*, and *best practices*

- Transformation Consciousness by focusing on *adaptability*, *innovation*, *employee empowerment*, *employee participation*, and *continuous learning*
  - Internal Cohesion Consciousness by developing a culture based on *shared values*, and a *shared vision* that engenders an organization-wide climate of *trust*
  - Making a Difference Consciousness by creating *strategic alliances* and *partnerships* with other organizations and the local community, as well as developing *mentoring*, *coaching*, and *leadership development* programs for employees
  - Service consciousness by focusing on *social responsibility*, *ethics*, and *sustainability*, and keeping a *long-term perspective* on their business and its impact on *future generations*, as well as embracing *compassion*, *humility*, and *forgiveness*

All these factors make an organization attractive (magnetic) to employees, customers, and investors.

Stakeholders

Conscious Capitalism leaders know the importance of taking into account *all* of their stakeholders. You're never going to become a premium brand by only focusing on the shareholders. The really important factors for long-term business success are the employees and customers, and often the vendors and community as well. Take care of them, and they will take care of you.

Any organization has multiple stakeholders, including customers, employees, suppliers, investors, partners, the community, and others. Some companies focus on their shareholders to the exclusion of everything else—these tend to be win-at-all cost companies. A conscious company, on the other hand, concentrates on the whole or integrated business ecosystem designed to create and optimize value for all of its stakeholders. It provides a proven and functional map for orienting the values of your employees, leaders, and stakeholders. More so, it offers an avenue to shape more supportive and productive relationships between them and a deeper rooting of your purpose throughout your company.

What B Corps Measure

It's important to note that what you decide to measure will define your outcomes. In the world of B Corps, for instance, there are roughly eighty different versions of the B Impact Assessment (BIA), as it customizes itself according to your company's size, industry, and geography. This widely used assessment includes around 200 questions that measure a company's performance in the areas of governance, workers, community, environment, and customers. If a company scores more than 80 points in the BIA and completes the rigorous verification process with B Lab, then it is eligible to certify. Recertification is required every three years.

One aspect that makes B Corp certification unique is that it includes a legal requirement: Certified B Corps must amend their governing documents (e.g., articles of incorporation, operating agreement, or other such foundational documents) to include stakeholder consideration. The reason behind this is to "correct" our economic system that currently prioritizes profits over everything else—by incorporating stakeholder consideration into its governing documents, a company can protect its values, purpose, and mission for the long run, even through changes in ownership.

This is the tool that Patagonia uses to measure success. Here is what Rose Marcario, CEO of Patagonia, had to say about the B Impact Assessment: "Although we submit to other audits of labor and environmental practices, the B Impact Assessment (a free tool that helps companies measure, compare, and improve their social and environmental performance) provides us with the only comprehensive view of our standing with all our stakeholders: owners, employees, customers, local communities, suppliers' communities, and the planet."[45]

The B Impact Assessment Sections

The BIA is divided into five different sections:

- **Governance:** Standards here relate to mission, stakeholder engagement, governance structure and controls, and transparency.
- **Workers:** The standards in this section look at how a company treats its employees, including the compensation practices, benefits, training, worker ownership, employee engagement and development, and work environment.
- **Community:** This section covers the company's impact on external community stakeholders, including suppliers, distributors, and the local economy and community, as well as the company's practices regarding diversity, job creation, civic engagement, and charitable giving.
- **Environment:** These standards relate to a company's direct and indirect environmental impacts.
- **Customers:** These standards relate to the impact that a business model has on customers, including underserved populations.

Ultimately, the BIA serves the brilliant dual purpose of operationalizing the often hard-to-define concepts of social and environmental responsibility while offering the opportunity for a deep-dive business analysis. Users of the BIA often report several "a-ha" moments while working through the assessment that inspire them to make meaningful changes in their businesses to benefit their stakeholders. The BIA has been used by more than 100,000 companies around the world. This global movement now includes more than 4,000 Certified B Corp companies in 77 countries and 153 industries, all sharing a single unifying goal "to redefine success in business."

If you want more insights and tools to define a measurement system for your business, I invite you to download the free *Beautiful Business Outcomes* workbook at www.the-beautiful-business.com.

The Beautiful Business Lexicon

Artistry — Is the natural human creative skill or ability to create something that has a high degree of quality, value, effect, and craftsmanship. Artistry is both the innate and learned skills to creatively adapt and respond with wholeheartedness in heart, mind, and soul to infuse more beauty through the felt and sensory experiences to evolve the work and the business at hand. In the business world and the world of work, it is the ability to act with creative or innovative response to the needs, challenges, and opportunities within and for the organization and the people and stakeholders associated with it. It is artistry that evolves the organization, and artistry that individuals employ to evolve themselves, and support in the evolution of those around them.

Evolved Leaders — Are individuals who are traveling a committed path to the continuous growth and evolution of themselves and for those around them—a path that considers and manages the interconnected nature of the beliefs, systems, processes, and multiple stakeholders in and around the business. Evolved Leaders are driven by and connected to a higher purpose and vision, who know that becoming the best leader they can be is an upward-spiral process they will never be fully complete. These leaders have consciously chosen to see and apply their roles to accelerate cultures of learning and growth in service to the business purpose and its related stakeholders. The role of the Evolved Leader is to set the purpose and vision, be a steward for the values, and to create the conditions in which the culture can thrive. Attributes of an Evolved Leader:

- Consistently demonstrate a high degree of internal (inner drivers and motivations) and external (the effects their actions, energy and words have on others) self-awareness
- Cultivates the ability to deeply listen and to notice the state and needs of the team
- Displays a fusion of courageous acts of both excellence and vulnerability—shows both their faults and gifts.
- Has the willingness to continually learn and improve.
- Demonstrates the recognition and orchestration of the interconnectedness of all stakeholders.
- Sets the purpose and vision for the team, identifies and lives the values, creates a psychological safe space and conditions for the team to thrive.

—

Brand Essence — synonym to Brand Purpose (see Purpose)

Leadership — Is the self-assigned, outside of role or title, ability to set a vision and create the conditions in which the team thrives and the goals are achieved.

Beauty — Is a felt sense that you or someone else experiences that comes from the core, the soul, and the essence of something, like a place, or a company. Beauty is derived from the value-system that sits in the heart of your business, vocation, and life. In the context of *The Beautiful Business*, beauty is a revolution of values that are inherited from the better angels of our nature and moves people from transactions to transcendent experiences. This is full-spectrum beauty.

Belief System — Is the way in which a culture (business, team, community, or collective) collectively constructs and aligns in the shaping of a model or framework for how it thinks about its driving motivations. In the context of this book, the belief system is the foundation to the Brand Belief Matrix.

Brand — The character of an organization that comes from the deeply held beliefs in action at the core of the business. This branded character in action leaves indelible impressions on all who come into contact with it, which comes from the intrinsic motivations and beliefs of the people inside the business which are consistently expressed through actions and expressions. In business, brand is the character of the organization that comes from its deeply held beliefs applied into consistent action that leaves an indelible and lasting impression on those who come into contact with it. (see Character)

—

Brand Belief Matrix — The unique fusion of defined and activated beliefs that a team, business, or culture holds as firmly held beliefs which are consistently put into action to clarify the work at hand which measurably benefits all stakeholders. The *Brand Belief Matrix* comes from the business belief system, which includes: purpose, vision, core values, and promise.

Business (also: **Corporation**, **Company**, or **Organization**) — A business is a value-driven, legal entity that comprises of the people who join together to create something of significant value that they cannot do on their own. It is derived from the Latin *corporare* meaning to 'combine in one body.' In this sense, a business, corporation, company, or organization, is a single, unified entity made of separate parts and functions—including people, systems, processes, sub-divisions, and governance—that fuses together through its common cause, driving beliefs and actions to do the work at hand which, in turn, creates value for all stakeholders.

Belonging — or ***True Belonging*** as defined by Brené Brown: "True belonging is the spiritual practice of believing in and belonging to yourself so deeply that you can share your most authentic self with the world and find sacredness in both being part of something and standing alone in the wilderness. True belonging doesn't require you the change who you are; it requires you to be who you are." In the workplace, belonging is the knowing and the felt sense of security and support when there is acceptance, inclusion, and identity for who people truly are. In order for people to feel like they belong, the environment (the culture, the community, or the workplace) needs to be designed and fostered to be a diverse and inclusive place.

—

Character — Is the sum of defining qualities that characterize a person, thing, or entity, such as a business that comes from the deeply held beliefs and consistent behaviors that are driven by these beliefs. The roots of *character* can be traced back to the Greek *charassein*, meaning "to sharpen, cut in furrows, or engrave." This word gave the Greeks *charaktēr*, a noun meaning "mark, distinctive quality."

Circle of Artistry — Is the ever-evolving and self-rejuvenating system of creation that artists, makers, craftspeople, entrepreneurs, and others use to create something that moves the world or an audience. The Circle of Artistry is comprised of five key stages: intention, creation, refinement, presentation or performance, and presence in receiving. Each stage builds on and informs the next, and it is a circle because each journey through the Circle of Artistry brings the artist back to the beginning intention stage.

Evolution — Is the ability to and process of adapting, changing, and growing in a positive or more useful direction. Evolution can be applied to our lives, our work and our business. Evolution is the vital process of gradual development and maturation of something—like a business, product, or life—from one form to an improved form. In the business world, evolution is the state change in the existing characteristics of the organization over time. It is the process in which the whole entity, including its interrelated parts, progresses.

Harmony — Is the sound or feeling of things that go together well, as in music that is a pleasing combination and progression of chords. While harmony is not possible at all times in business, it is something that a business cans strive towards. Because much of business success depends on our ability to unite in the common work at hand in service to others, harmony becomes highly beneficial in the degree to which we can align for the mutual success of the business for all its stakeholders. Synonyms for *harmony* include accord, cooperation, like-mindedness, unanimity, and integrity.

Integrity — Is a personality or character trait that creates the personal inner and outer sense of "wholeness" which is derived from the alignment of our beliefs and behaviors. Integrity is consistency of actions, values, methods, measures, principles, expectations, and outcomes. The degree of our integrity defines, to a large extent, our character. Integrity comes from the Latin *integritas*, meaning wholeness.

Magnetism — Is the power to attract, to bond, to invite. It refers to the attraction to iron and other metals in electric currents and magnets, or to the other kind of attraction—where people want to be close to each other. Magnetism in business "pulls" or "attracts" customers toward your brand, your business and your offerings by using the beliefs and value system along with the value of your product or service offerings which provide prospects with engaging communications they're attracted to. Magnetism in marketing or sales is the alignment of a value and values with your prospects and customers.

Marketing — Is the expression and articulation of the value of the company's products or services. It is the series of story-telling processes employed through all media touchpoints which consistently expresses the value customers will get through a win-win relationship with the company, brand, product, or service.

Outcomes — Is the measurable and non-measurable results that come from the designed and unified efforts of the work that the business does.

Purpose — Is the business' reason for being beyond making money which acts as driving motivation and through-line for why the company exists. Our purpose, when properly defined and activated consistently, will move a business through struggles, obstacles, and challenges and it is driven by an intrinsic force within the heart of the organization. A higher purpose, one that is built with integrity, is essential for having love infused within the business. The business or brand purpose is one that aligns emotionally to all stakeholders connected to the business.

Promise — Is the explicit, valuable, and measurable benefit or outcome that your customers will consistently receive from your company's products or services. The three components of a valuable promise are: Explicit: you clearly state it so people understand it; Valuable: it offers some clear value to the people you're promising; Measurable: your company holds itself accountable through measurement systems to ensure you're living up to your stated promise.

Sales — Is either helping or serving people who will gain value from the offered products or services of the business. The sales process is the series of conversation in which the business positions, vets, values, and converts business opportunities.

Self-Awareness — Is the conscious knowledge of one's own character, feelings, motives, and desires, both through our internal beliefs, drivers, and motivations, and externally on how our attitude, energy, and actions effect those around us.

Spirituality — As defined by Brené Brown: "Recognizing and celebrating that we are all inextricably connected to each other by a power greater than all of us, and that our connection to that power and to one another is grounded in love and belonging. Practicing spirituality brings a sense of perspective, meaning, and purpose to our lives."[46]

Value — Is the fair and equitable exchange in return for good, services, or money. Value is the fair exchange of energy flow to and from customers and businesses. It is also the principle of quality that is desirable, fair, and valuable. Value, in the marketplace, can also be defined as a common bond of values that fosters ties between the people associated (stakeholders) with the business.

Values — Are the beliefs that the organization holds as most vital and important as team members go about living and working in their daily lives and work. Living through values means that the team and individuals act in accordance with the values, especially when faced with difficult choices, big decisions, or conflict. Organizational values, when consistently put into action, create an operating system for the culture. Values are defined through actionable beliefs and the behavior that the organization wants to reinforce when the individuals and the team is performing at its best. Values define how the people in the organization unite through behaviors that strive toward the common cause (purpose) of the business.

Vision — Is what the world will look like, feel like, and be changed as the company goes about achieving its Purpose.

Acknowledgments

It's not an underestimation to point out that this book has been many years, maybe a lifetime, in the making. There are countless people who've made it possible. I hold deep gratitude in my heart for all who have touched my world—good, bad, or otherwise. I am especially grateful to the following people.

Chris. Our path together has been long and beautiful and the privilege of my life. We've known each other since our twenties, and life gets richer as each year passes. You keep my head pointed in the right direction and my heart grounded in what matters most. Our morning conversations orient the compass of my life. You've made me an exponentially better person for the love and life we share.

My sons, Evan and Ellis. I am so proud of you both. You are so very easy to love. You have blossomed into young men with great character. You have made me immeasurably better by simply being your dad. You have helped me live up to the daily mantra I shared with you each day as I dropped you off at school when you were younger.

Mom and Dad. As time passes, my appreciation for what you've provided for me and my siblings grows in understanding and appreciation. You each, in your own way, trusted me to follow my uncertain and unpredictable path through life. I'm quite certain you scratched your heads about my choices in life many times, and I was likely the cause for some sleepless nights. You have my deepest gratitude.

My Studio mates: Libby Wagner and Owen Ó Súilleabháin. You have encouraged me to put my artistry into everything I do. Your caring words, your soul-filled music, your courageous hearts stand side by side with mine. I am forever indebted to you for our beautiful work together.

Denise Lee Yohn. Our mutual collaborations and co-guidance have both challenged my thinking (for the better) and kept me grounded in the "fusion" of our vocational and spiritual paths we each travel. Our conversations inspire me to be more me; for that, I am forever grateful.

My Elevation Collective colleagues: Chris Cooper, Gene Early, Sarah Santacroce, Elisabet Hern, Hilary Wilson, John Jennings, and Mike Mooney. Our space-holding and inquiry work within our leadership circle is, no doubt, making better leaders of each of us and will echo and ring in immeasurable ways. Our questions and the variety of perspectives that encircle them continue to shore up the foundations of my world. Your fingerprints exist on the pages of this book and especially around leadership.

David Whyte. I suspect you have only a small inkling of the impact that your firm voice and beautiful questions have had on me during our time together in Whidbey Island at *Invitas*, adventures through Tuscany, and the many times I soaked up your words and stories. I am grateful for your "clear mind and wild heart."

—

My clients. I have been honored to work with so many of you passionate, thoughtful, and driven leaders. By entrusting me to help guide and grow your businesses, you've challenged me to be better at what I do and continually improve the manner in which I serve. Thank you for allowing me to serve you and inviting me to influence the trajectory of your business and life.

My artist and designer brothers and sisters. You put poetry in my heart that I live with each and every day. You help me see a brighter world by the beauty you offer others. You remind me that we stand in a lineage of artistic and creative past that I do my best to pass on to current and future generations.

My influential thinkers and writers. Many of you I have the honor to know, some I don't (at least not yet). Your thinking and writing make me a better thinker, better consultant, better adviser, better artist. Leisa Peterson. Jenny Blake. Dorie Clark. Gay Hendricks. Marty Neumeier. Jonathan Fields. Debbie Millman. Chip Conley. David Baker. Ryan Holiday. Greg McKeown. Adam Grant. Seth Godin. Sam Harris. Tim Ferriss. To name a few.

Joe Scorsone. As my formative graduate school professor, you (almost) always believed in me. Your way of forming questions about why the work matters encouraged me to think and rethink time and time again.

Mr. Bartoli. I haven't known you since my days at Laura Little Elementary School, but your encouragement made a world of difference to me. You are the mark of a great teacher, who sees and encourages young people to live their dreams.

—

Flip Brown. It's been said that the best feedback you'll ever get is criticism from people who have your best interests at heart. Your comments and recommendations to this book's manuscript made for a more inclusive and diverse representation of the people and companies I highlighted. I am deeply appreciative for our friendship and for your concerned feedback.

Heather Paulsen. I deeply appreciate you lending me and this book your expertise in understanding and articulating the world of B Corps. You helped to make the "Outcomes that Matter" chapter clearer and more accurate. For these contributions and your kindness, I am in your debt.

The RTC/CCP team. Your enthusiastic embracing of this unusual book stoked an ember in my belly and created fire. Your gentle but clear guidance helped me take the (many) rough drafts of this book and make it better each step of the way. Your editorial guidance helped to clarify the purpose of and the audience for this book. To Corey: Our conversations sharpened my thinking and lightened my heart. To Agata: Your editorial guidance and the "artistry" conversations made this book immeasurably better.

With deep gratitude—I couldn't, and likely wouldn't, have done it without you all.

Endnotes

1 James Clear, "3-2-1: Creative Ideas, Wealth, and Making Life a Celebration," James Clear [personal website], May 7, 2020, https://jamesclear.com/3-2-1/may-7-2020.

2 Carl Sagan, *Pale Blue Dot: A Vision of the Human Future in Space* (New York: Ballantine Books, 1994), 6.

3 David Whyte, "Working Together," *River Flow: New & Selected Poems*. Printed with permission from Many Rivers Press, www.davidwhyte.com. © Many Rivers Press, Langley, WA USA.

4 David Whyte, "Sometimes," *Everything Is Waiting for You*. Printed with permission from Many Rivers Press, www.davidwhyte.com. © Many Rivers Press, Langley, WA USA.

5 *Dead Poet's Society*, directed by Peter Weir (Touchstone Pictures, 1989).

6 Martin Luther King Jr., "Beyond Vietnam," April 4, 1967, Stanford University, transcript and audio 1:02:20, https://kinginstitute.stanford.edu/king-papers/documents/beyond-vietnam.

7 James Shield, "Identity Politics, Social Media, and Tribalism: An Interview with Jonathan Haidt," The RSA, December 7, 2018, https://www.thersa.org/discover/publications-and-articles/rsa-blogs/2018/12/haidt.

8 David W. Nicholson, *Philosophy of Education in Action: An Inquiry-Based Approach* (New York: Routledge, 2016), 48.

9 https://hbr.org/2018/01/how-and-where-diversity-drives-financial-performance

10 Brené Brown, *The Gifts of Imperfection: Let Go of Who You Think You're Supposed to Be and Embrace Who You Are* (Center City, MN: Hazelden, 2010), 25.

11 Brené Brown, *Braving the Wilderness: The Quest for True Belonging and the Courage to Stand Alone* (New York: Random House, 2019), 160.

12 "Discovering Your Purpose with Steven Morris & Chris Cooper," January 15, 2021, in *The Business Elevation Show with Chris Cooper*, podcast, audio, 56:13, https://www.iheart.com/podcast/256-the-business-elevation-sho-31080304/episode/discovering-your-purpose-with-steven-morris-76302869/.

13   Krista Tippett, "Seth Godin: Life, the Internet, and Everything," *On Being with Krista Tippet*, aired January 24, 2013, https://onbeing.org/programs/seth-godin-life-the-internet-and-everything-sep2018/.

14   Chad Gordon, "The Importance of Self-Awareness with Tasha Eurich," Blanchard LeaderChat, February 1, 2019, https://leaderchat.org/2019/02/01/the-importance-of-self-awareness-with-tasha-eurich/.

15   Simon Sinek, *The Infinite Game*, Simon Sinek, https://simonsinek.com/product/the-infinite-game/#:~:text=In%20finite%20games%2C%20like%20football,there%20is%20no%20defined%20endpoint.

16   Simon Sinek, *The Infinite Game*, Simon Sinek, https://simonsinek.com/product/the-infinite-game/#:~:text=In%20finite%20games%2C%20like%20football,there%20is%20no%20defined%20endpoint.

17   Robert Greene, *Mastery* (New York: Viking, 2012), 180.

18   Victor Frankl, *Man's Search for Meaning* (Boston: Beacon Press, 2014), x.

19   Mary Olivier, "Poem 133: The Summer Day," Library of Congress, https://www.loc.gov/programs/poetry-and-literature/poet-laureate/poet-laureate-projects/poetry-180/all-poems/item/poetry-180-133/the-summer-day/.

20   Brené Brown, "The Power of Vulnerability – Brené Brown," August 15, 2013, YouTube video, 21:47, https://www.youtube.com/watch?v=sXSjc-pbXk4.

21   Judith Pickering, *Being in Love: Therapeutic Pathways Through Psychological Obstacles to Love* (New York: Routledge, 2008), 18.

22   "Bretha Comaithchesa: 'Judgements of Neighbourhood,'" Codecs, https://www.vanhamel.nl/codecs/Bretha_comaithchesa.

23   Hsiao-yun Chu and Roberto G. Trujillo, *New Views on R. Buckminster Fuller* (Stanford: Stanford University Press, 2009), 90.

24   Hilda Emery Davis and Garry Davis, *Letters to World Citizens* (South Burlington, VT: World Government House, 2000), 101.

25   *Uncovering Talent: A New Model of Inclusion*, Deloitte Development, 2019, https://www2.deloitte.com/us/en/pages/about-deloitte/articles/covering-in-the-workplace.html.

26   Ryan Holiday, *The Obstacle Is the Way: The Timeless Art of Turning Trials into Triumph* (New York: Portfolio/Penguin, 2014), 16.

27   David Whyte, *Crossing the Unknown Sea* (New York: Riverhead Books, 2002).

28   Rainer Maria Rilke, "The Swan," in *Selected Poems of Rainer Maria Rilke*, trans. Robert Bly (Paradise, CA: Paw Prints, 2008).

29   *2019 Edelman Trust Barometer,* Edelman, 2019, https://www.edelman
     .com/research/trust-barometer-expectations-for-ceos-2019.

30   Andrew T. Carswell, ed., *The Encyclopedia of Housing,* second
     edition (New York: SAGE Publications, 2012).

31   "Historical Households Tables," US Census Bureau, December 2020,
     https://www.census.gov/data/tables/time-series/demo/families
     /households.html.

32   Marin Luther King Jr., *The Radical King,* ed. Cornel West (Boston:
     Beacon Press, 2015), 78.

33   *Dead Poet's Society,* dir. Peter Weir.

34   "Gratitude, Not 'Gimme,' Makes for More Satisfaction, Study Finds,"
     Science Daily, March 31, 2014, https://www.sciencedaily.com/releases
     /2014/03/140331180613.htm.

35   Abraham Maslow, "A Theory of Human Motivation," in *The Maslow
     Business Reader,* ed. Deborah C. Stephens (New York: John Wiley
     & Sons, 2000), 261.

36   Chip Conley, *Peak: How Great Companies Get Their Mojo from
     Maslow* (Hoboken, NJ: John Wiley & Sons, 2017), xxi.

37   Conley, *Peak,* 11.

38   Abraham Maslow, *Future Visions: The Unpublished Papers of
     Abraham Maslow,* ed. Edward Hoffman (Thousand Oaks, CA:
     SAGE Publications, 1996).

39   Brown, *Braving the Wilderness,* 34.

40   Pamela M. Kato, Steve W. Cole, Andrew S. Bradlyn, and Brad
     H. Pollock, "A Video Game Improves Behavioral Outcomes in
     Adolescents and Young Adults With Cancer: A Randomized Trial,"
     Pediatrics 122, no. 2 (August 2008): e305–e317, https://pediatrics
     .aappublications.org/content/122/2/e305.

41   "Conscious Capitalist Credo," Conscious Capitalism,
     https://www.consciouscapitalism.org/credo.

42   Angela Duckworth, *Grit: The Power of Passion and Perseverance*
     (New York: Scribner, 2016).

43   David Selinger, "Data Driven: What Amazon's Jeff Bezos Taught
     Me About Running a Company," Entrepreneur, September 11, 2014,
     https://www.entrepreneur.com/article/237326.

44   Selinger, "Data Driven."

45   "Completing the B Impact Assessment," Cultivating Capital,
     accessed February 26, 2021, https://www.cultivatingcapital.com
     /completing-b-impact-assessment/.

46   Brown, *The Gifts of Imperfection,* 45.

Steven Morris helps business leaders build unignorable brands, cultures, and businesses through his work as an advisor, author, and speaker. He has worked with business leaders from Samsung, Sony, Habitat for Humanity, Amazon, International Trademark Association, NFL, MLB, and over 250 other brands over his more than 25 years in business. He reaches more than 25,000 readers through his blog and also has written about brands, innovation, and culture as a contributing writer for *Retail Observer*, *Business Week*, *Brand Week*, *Conscious Company Magazine*, *Communication Arts*, *HOW Magazine*, and *MarketingProfs*.

When he is not supporting leaders in building beautiful brands and businesses, Steven explores his fascination with art and beauty as an artist, designer, outdoor enthusiast, surfer, and beekeeper. To learn more about Steven and his work, visit Matter Consulting (https://matterco.co/).

ELEVATE HUMANITY THROUGH BUSINESS.

Conscious Capitalism, Inc., supports a global community of business leaders dedicated to elevating humanity through business via their demonstration of purpose beyond profit, the cultivation of conscious leadership and culture throughout their entire ecosystem, and their focus on long-termism by prioritizing stakeholder orientation instead of shareholder primacy. We provide mid-market executives with innovative learning exchanges, transformational storytelling training, and inspiring conference experiences all designed to level-up their business operations and collectively demonstrate capitalism as a powerful force for good when practiced consciously.

We invite you, either as an individual or as a business, to join us and contribute your voice. Learn more about the global movement at www.consciouscapitalism.org.

CPSIA information can be obtained
at www.ICGtesting.com
Printed in the USA
LVHW021058021121
702217LV00010B/244/J